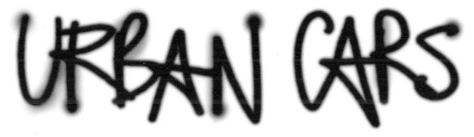

BROOKLYN

DOUGLAS LJUNGKVIST

WITH AN INTRODUCTION BY DEAN JOHNSON

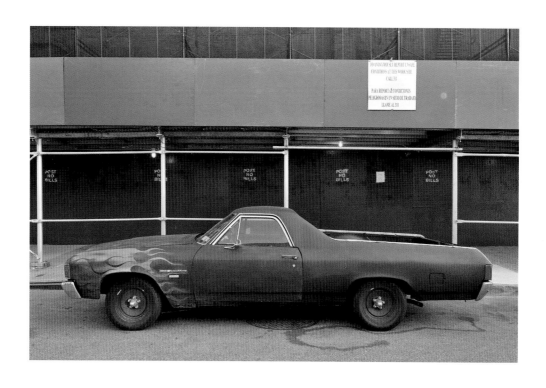

ABOUT THE ARTIST

Since 2007 I've been photographing vintage cars, mostly in Brooklyn's urban and industrial landscapes. The work has matured into a cohesive typology scheduled for publication in the Fall of 2018.

The project is a study of form, design, and beauty, documenting cars mostly from the 1960's and 1970's. The cars are photographed in a similar way to formal portraits, in profile and isolated from people and other cars. The visual relationship between the cars and their environment is more important to me than the brand, model, production year, or engine size.

I suspect my process is similar to a nature photographer looking for exotic animals to photograph in the wild. It's a bit like looking for a needle in a haystack. Whether on my scooter or on foot, I've perfected a one second glance down a block looking for unusual shapes or colors to identify something to add to the collection. I've even followed a few of them on my scooter until they parked and the owner walked away.

American cars of this era are still popular for their (masculine) aesthetics and raw power. They were built with individual expression in mind, to be seen and heard, at a time when everything was big and bold. As mechanical cars they are fairly easy to maintain and tinker with for hobbyists. The European cars in the collection reflect longevity and craftsmanship, attributes that are rare in today's modern and generically designed cars.

The work is also a celebration of 1970's vernacular color photography and the freedom, expression, and adventure that the automobile represented in American popular culture at a time when people didn't worry about the price of gasoline.

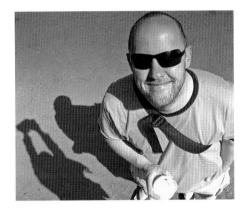

INTRODUCTION BY DEAN JOHNSON

The motor car has always promoted a spirit of freedom and independence and nowhere is that more formally written into the very fabric of the nation than America.

Since the horse took a back seat, the automotive industry has continued to evolve, but the pages of this book take a look under the hood of an era unto itself. From the fabulously fendered Chevys and Plymouths of the 1950s and 1960s, through the restrained, almost apologetic (by American standards), cars of the 1970s oil crisis, to the often poorly built and ill-conceived designs of the 1980s when manufacturers bolted on more plastic cladding than an out-of-favor reality TV star.

New York, and Brooklyn in particular, offers a unique window into America's automotive melting pot. Where Cadillacs brush shoulders with Volvos and multicolored school buses stand tall with VW Campers, these streets not only reveal a unique mix of vehicles, but the cars highlight the true nature and diversity of the neighborhood.

In the age of the smartphone, everyone has a camera in his or her pocket. We all have the power to capture the moment but Instagram and Snapchat filters don't deliver the essential skill of the real master photographer – a keen eye. Douglas Ljungkvist demonstrates not only this ability but something much deeper.

In his own words, he thinks he's more like a nature photographer hunting down his subjects, capturing them in their native habitat. Setting means nothing without a subject and these cars need their surroundings to feel at home. Ljungkvist shows us he's a master of composition by not simply marrying the two, but setting a scene in each fleeting moment.

Life happens in and around cars. It happens because of cars. They can be the ultimate statement of intent and capture or enhance a personality, or they can blend seamlessly into the background, becoming the very infrastructure and fabric of society.

We're heading toward an era where ownership and driving are things a generation will merely talk about as quaint idiosyncrasies of a bygone age. I don't just like cars, I love them, so I'm not here to sell the idea of the automotive future, but it's coming, like it or not – just not tomorrow, and not necessarily to the script everyone seems hellbent on following.

Right now, car design is still an important factor when considering which vehicle sits on our driveway, makes the school run, or parks outside our offices. Personality is still relevant – ours and our cars, but this won't always be the case.

Auto manufacturers now refer to 'mobility' rather than the specifics of cars or transport because we're already thinking about the journey and how we access the means to deliver ourselves rather than exactly what's responsible for doing so.

Future generations won't talk about their first car, they'll recount what happened in and around their first Uber ride. They won't look back and reminisce about the daily routine of service trucks, emergency vehicles or the time Mrs. Taylor from apartment 1B left the brake off her '81 Impala and it buried itself in the local deli.

Sure, we'll talk about the stories behind the journeys, but the visual reference won't have the same role to play.

A book like this is important because it preserves the things we would otherwise look back on and think weren't a priority. The small details. The dents, the scratches, the street art, the signs and sights that make this a book about the living, breathing population of a vibrant neighborhood and how the vehicles played their part, not the other way around.

You'll find walls full of books on the achievements of five-time Formula 1 Champion Fangio, or the evolution of aerodynamics, or the Italian designers that drove a creative revolution. But you won't find rust, you'll struggle to spot a dented fender and you won't stumble upon the things that make you smile on a personal level as they do here – because these cars meant something to us, as individuals and as a community. They take a different highway to the monumental automotive journeys recounted a thousand times because these vehicles tell our stories on a molecular level.

How they drove and what drove them are secondary to how they looked and lived.

My love affair with cars began with film and TV, and it was always about the story, how the car enhanced the narrative. Steve McQueen's '69 Mustang leaping into hearts and minds on the streets of San Francisco, Starsky and Hutch's Gran Torino smoking sideways round corners, Burt Reynolds making the Trans Am cool before handing that on to the Hoff with K.I.T.T., The Dukes of Hazard even managing to (briefly) distract me from Daisy with a bright orange Charger!

These cars held a fascination for me because of their sporting intent and instilled in me a love of cars that make a statement and delivered personality in spades. But it wasn't all about speed and American muscle cars – I still loved Columbo's battered Peugeot or Herbie the Beetle giving us the first hint of the future. He was after all an autonomous car, even before K.I.T.T. hit the road!

These vehicles became as familiar travelling companions on my TV screen as my father's series of Ford Escorts throughout the same period. Cars are amazing things that attach themselves to memories like music evokes the sights, sounds and emotions of our lives and loves. We spend such a significant part of our existence in them, so why wouldn't they?

Like my European take on the American cars of film and TV, one of the fascinating things about this book is the global significance of the vehicles featured. VW Campers and Beetles, Volvo 245s, a BMW 2002Tii, Datsun 240Z and a Citroën 2CV! They all made their journey to Brooklyn and each has a story to tell – in many instances, one of survival.

With *Urban Cars Brooklyn,* Ljungkvist breathes life into a range of vehicles on their home turf, not the one deemed most appropriate by an ad agency or even the owners themselves. This is raw visual storytelling without all the words fighting to get in the way.

All offer that soul-searching American freedom, a level of independence with the simplest of remits – get me from A to B, some offering the promise of C, but all undeniably unique. This isn't a story of mass production, but one of mass adoption and every car on every page drops straight into history. A rich history that refuses to clear the road, because sometimes progress just isn't as much fun.

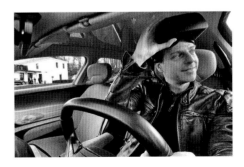

WELCOME T

BROOKLYN

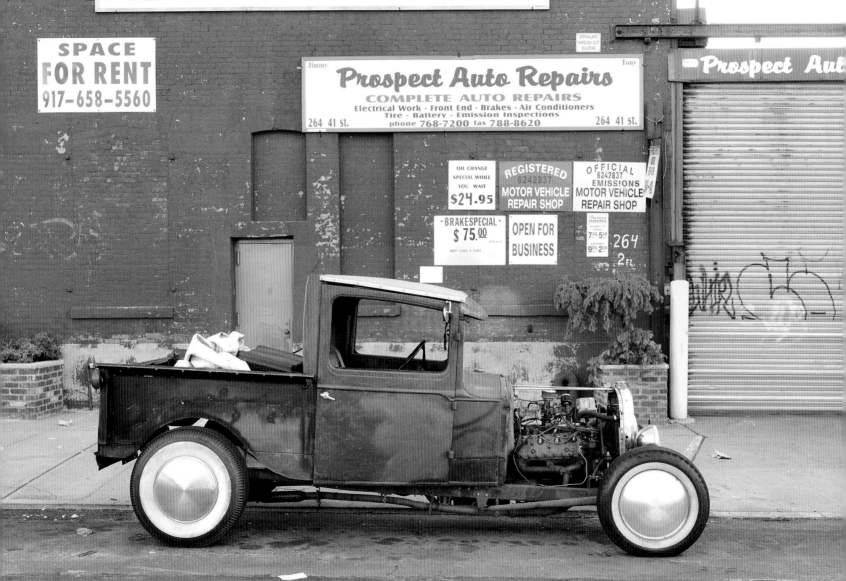

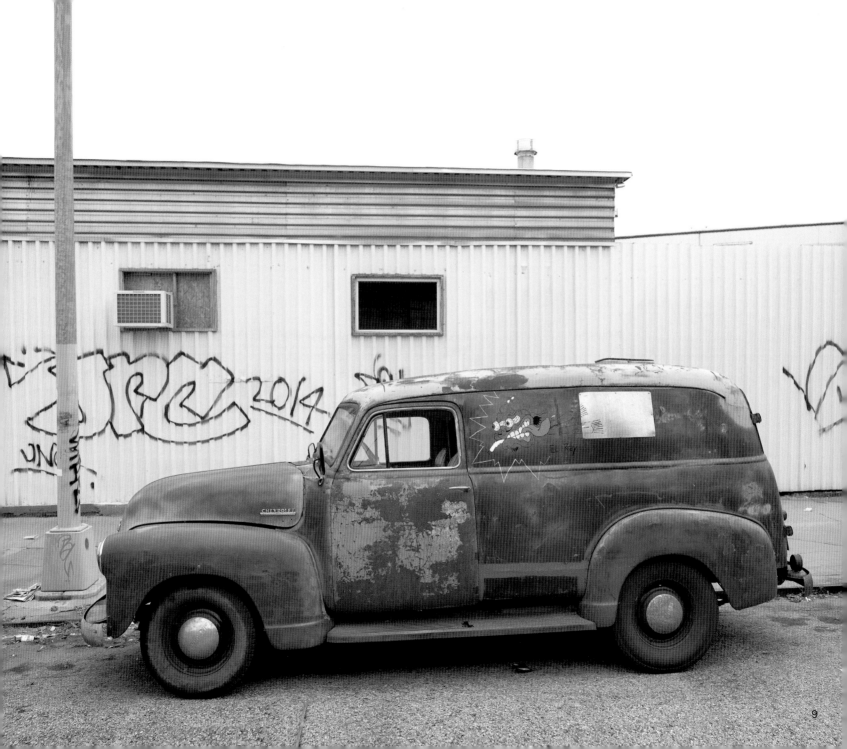

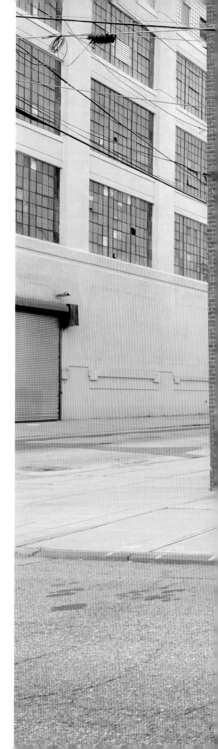

"ONE PERSON'S
CAR IS ANOTHER
PERSON'S SCENERY."

JONATHAN IVE

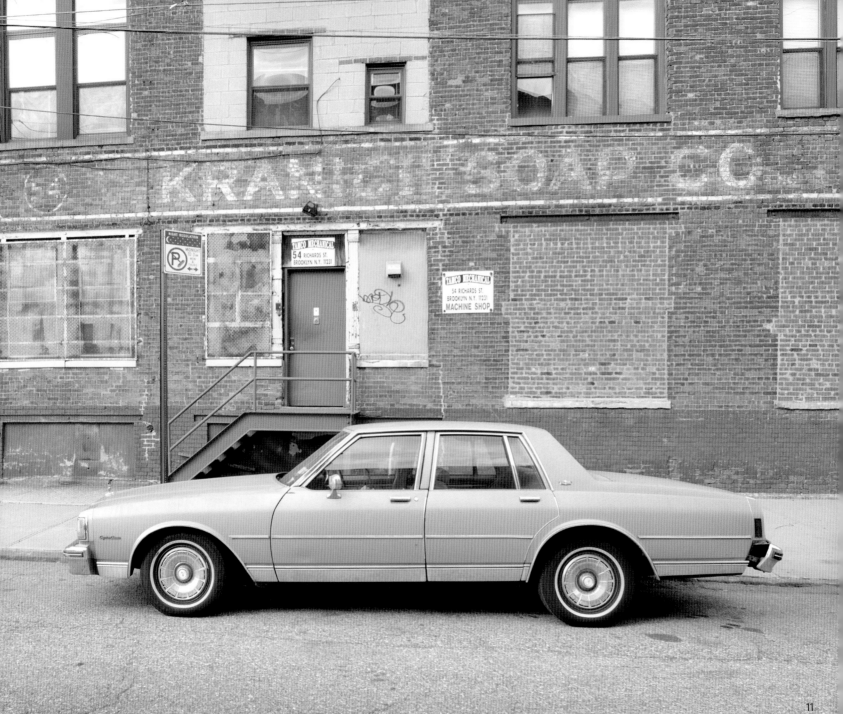

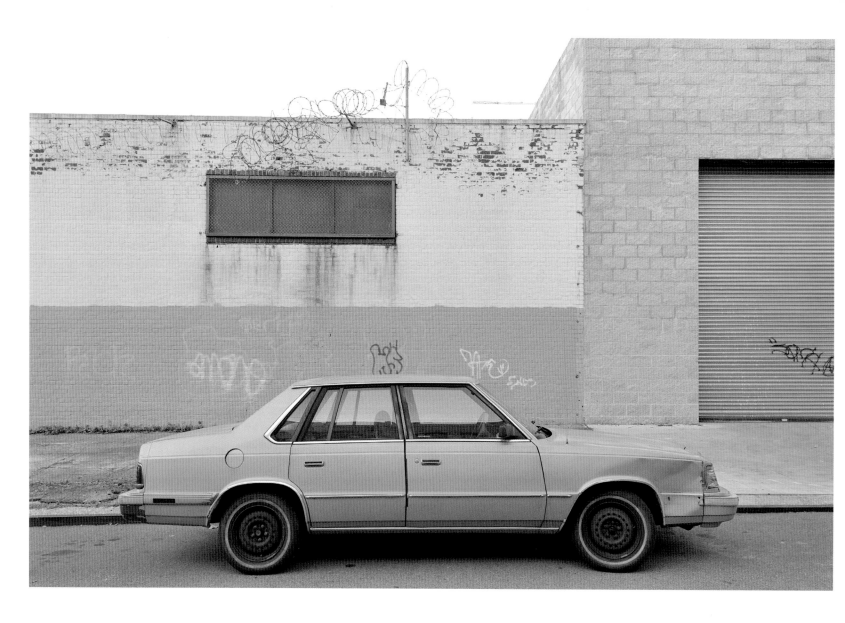

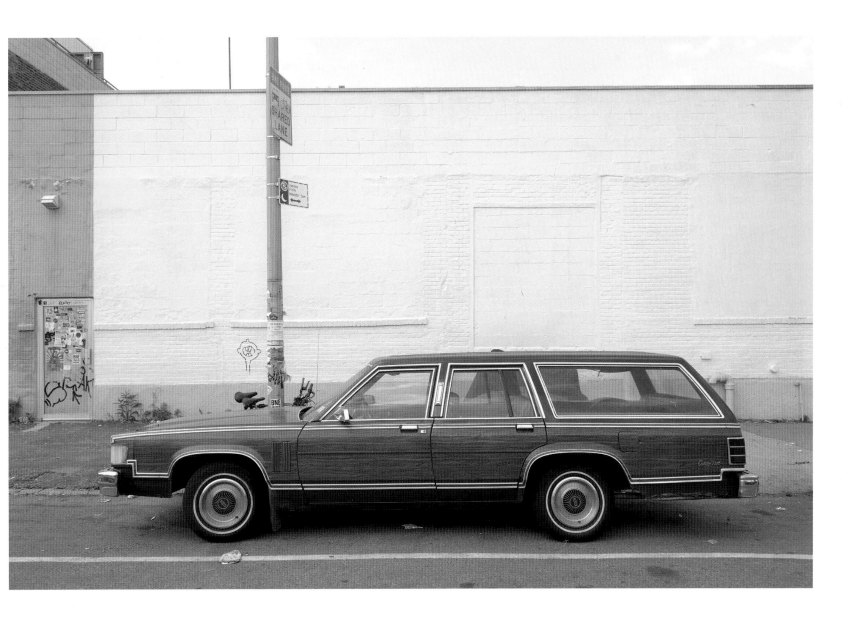

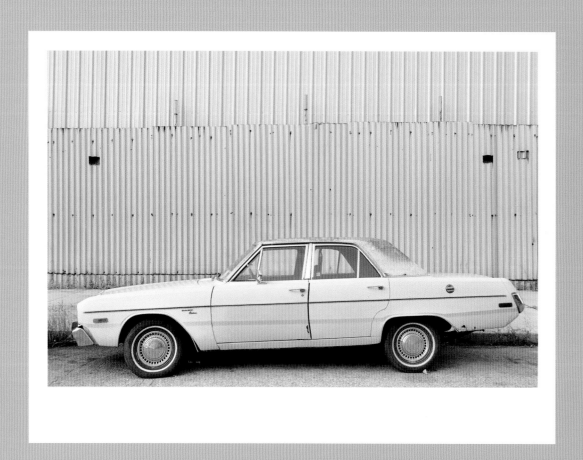

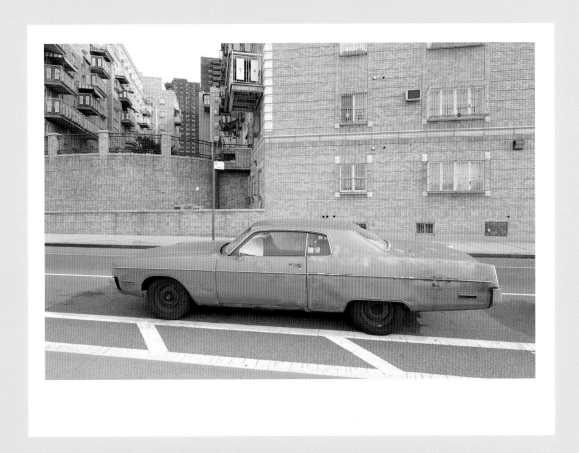

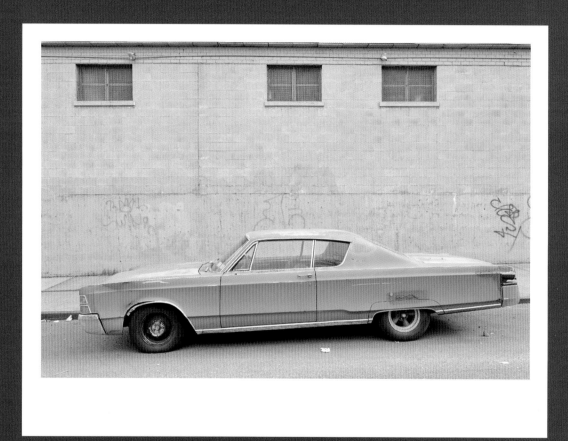

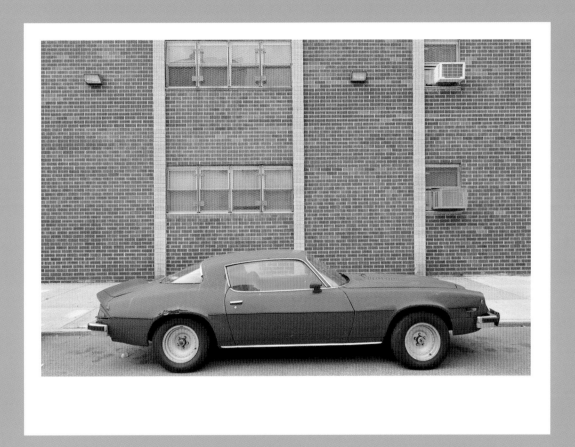

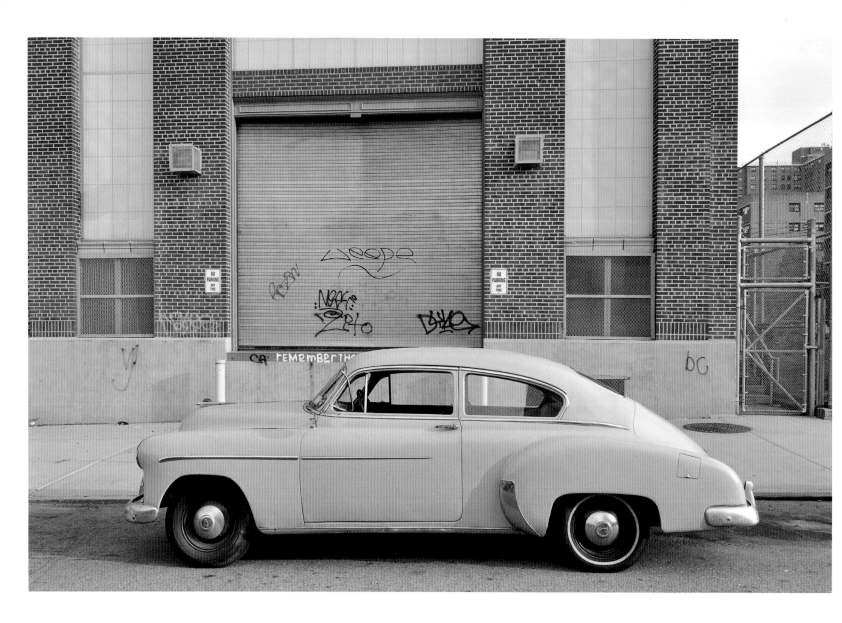

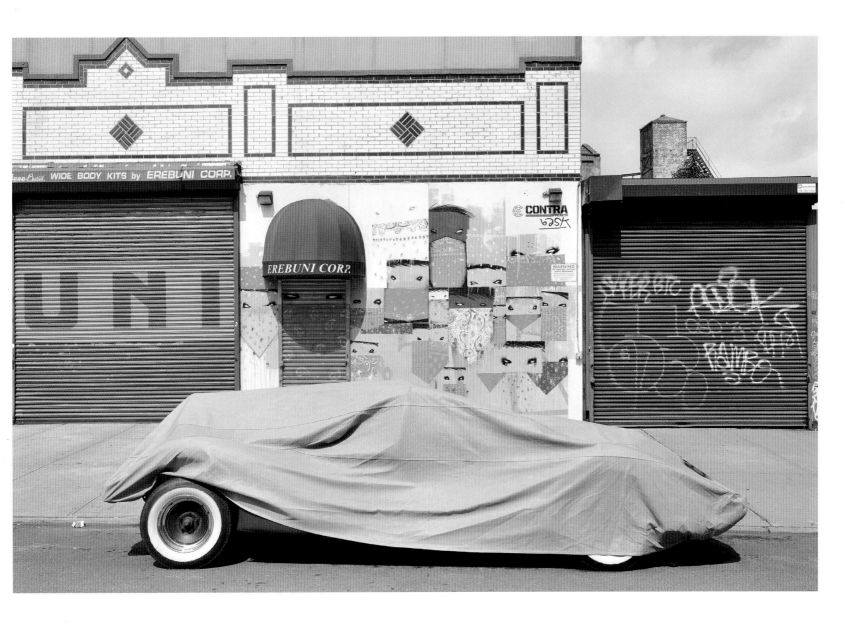

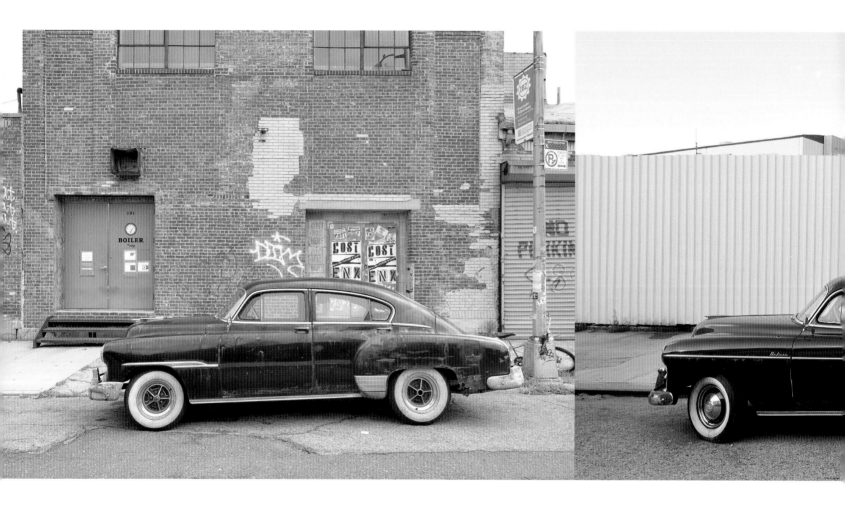

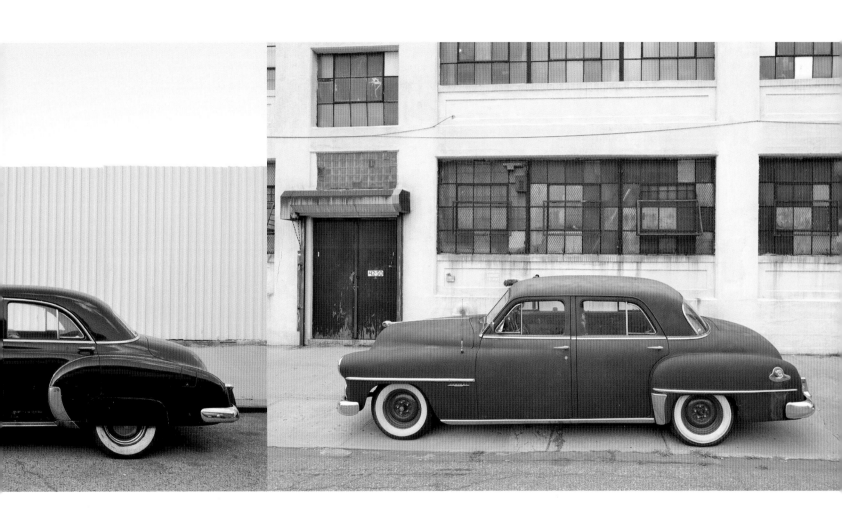

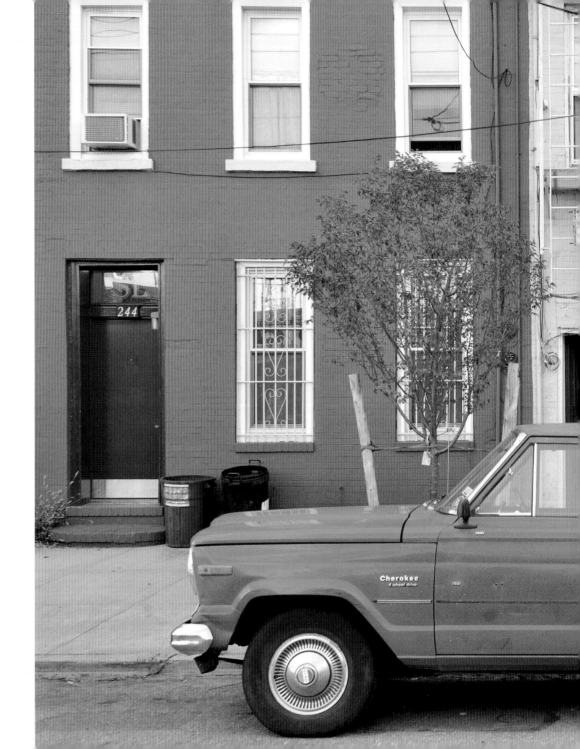

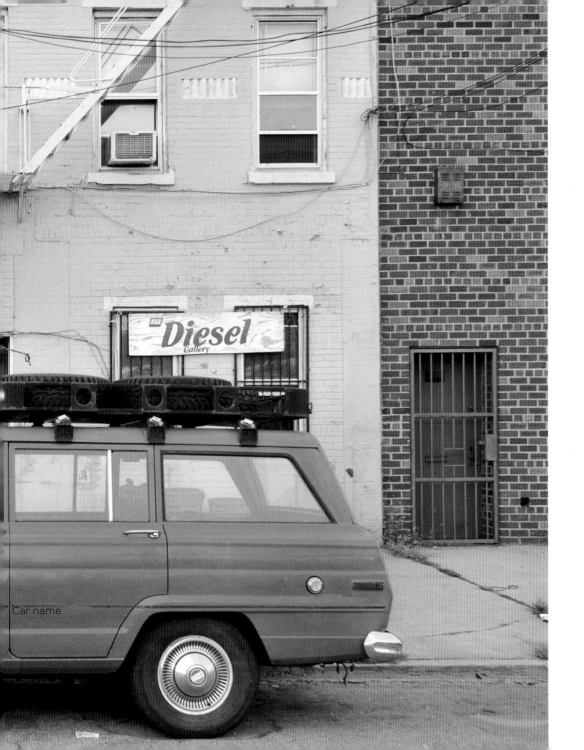

Car name

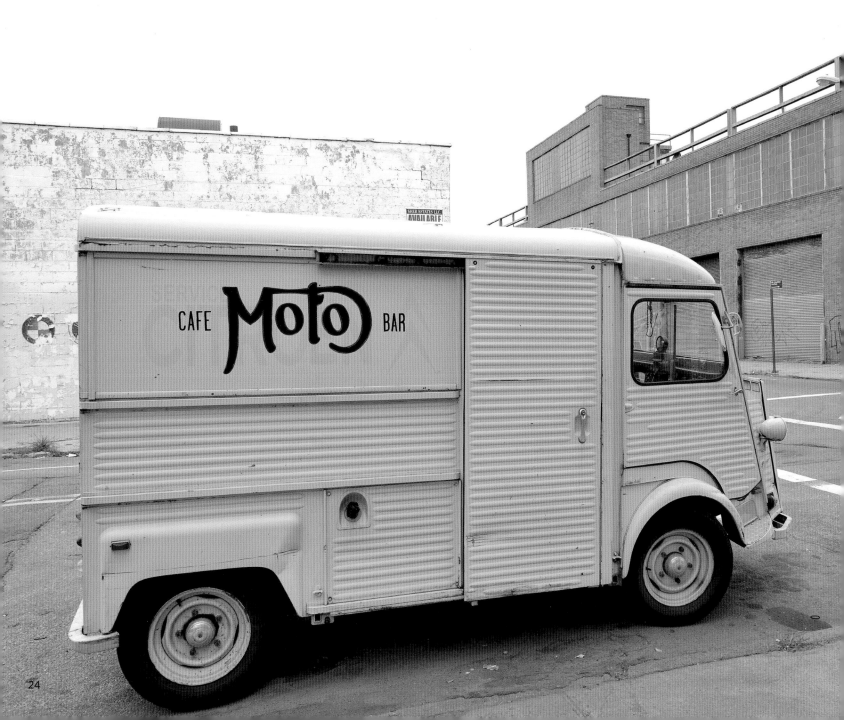

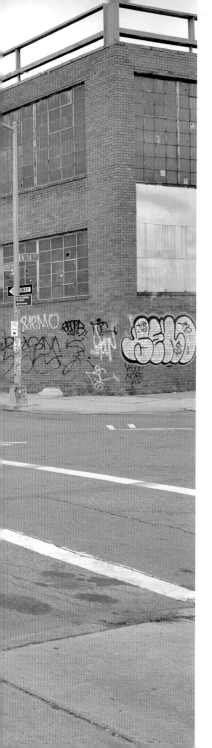

"EVERYONE'S NICER
TO ME WHEN I'M
IN YELLOW."

CAM

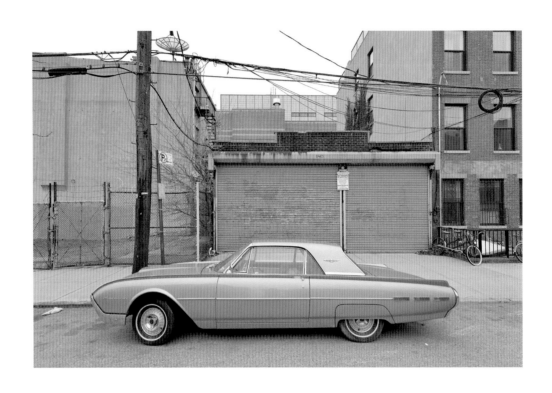

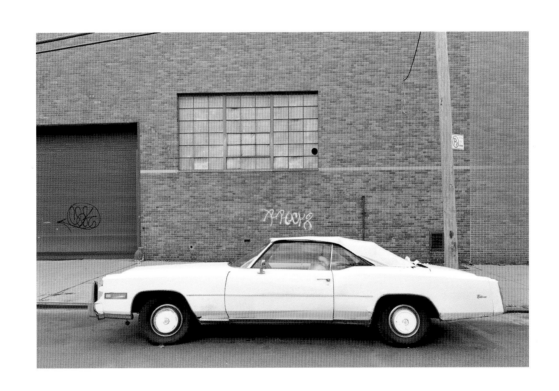

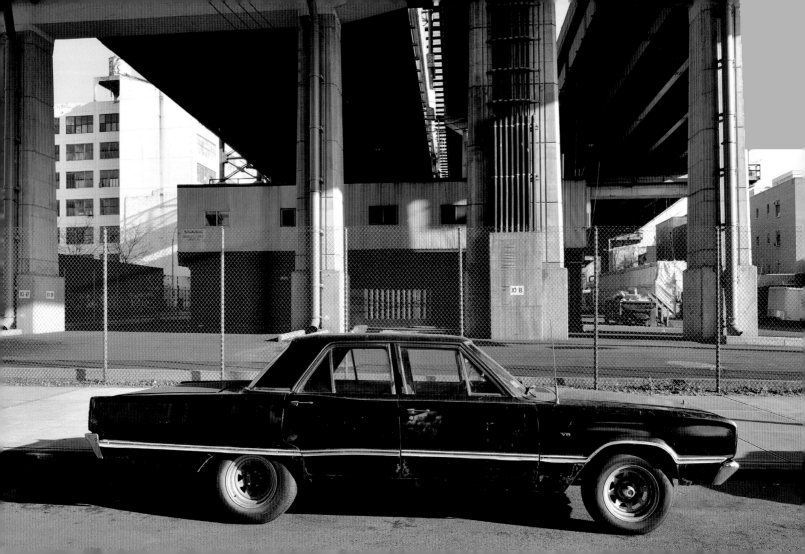

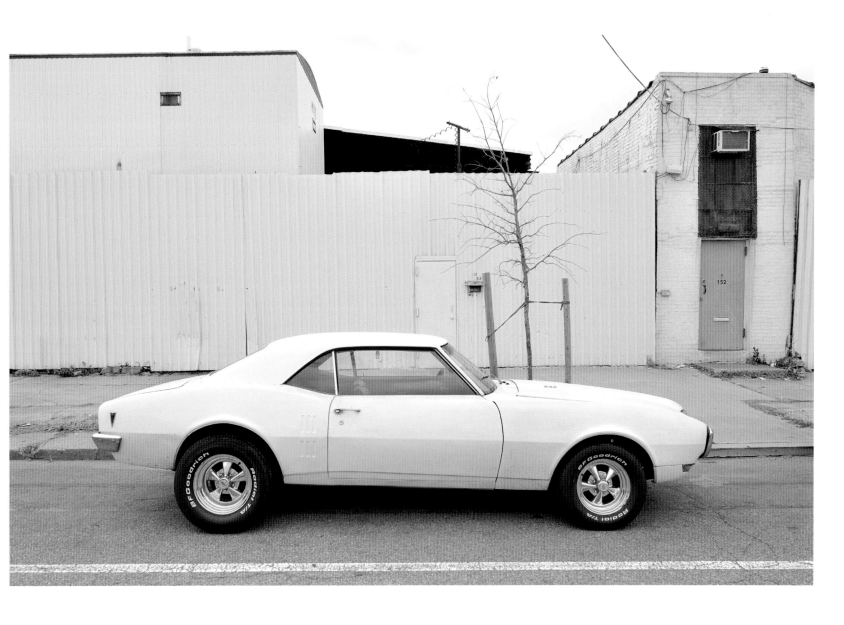

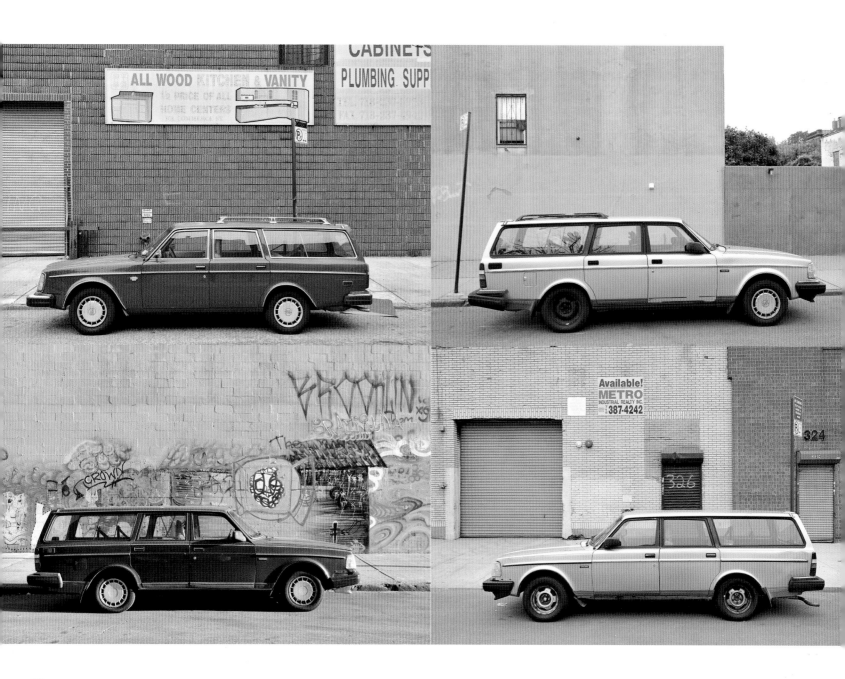

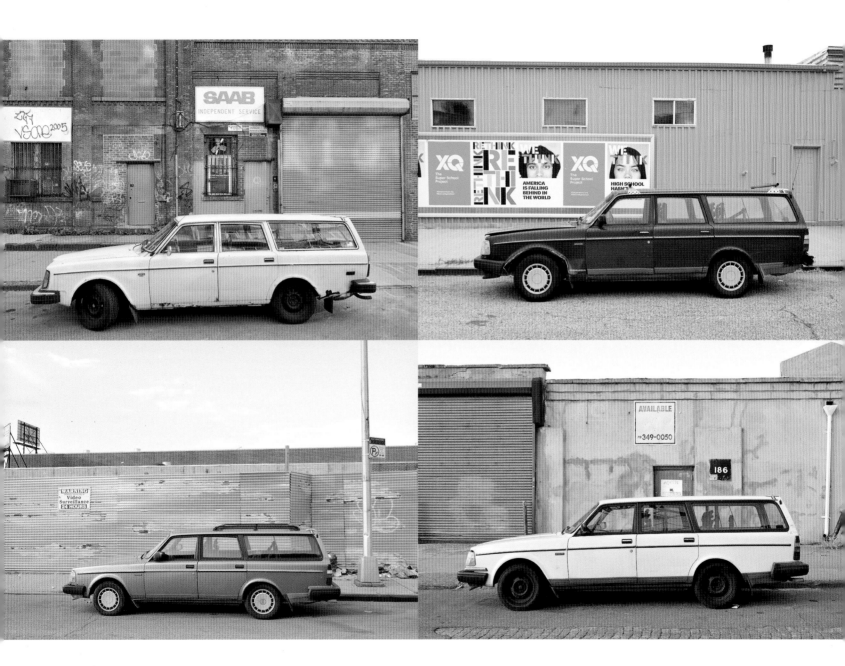

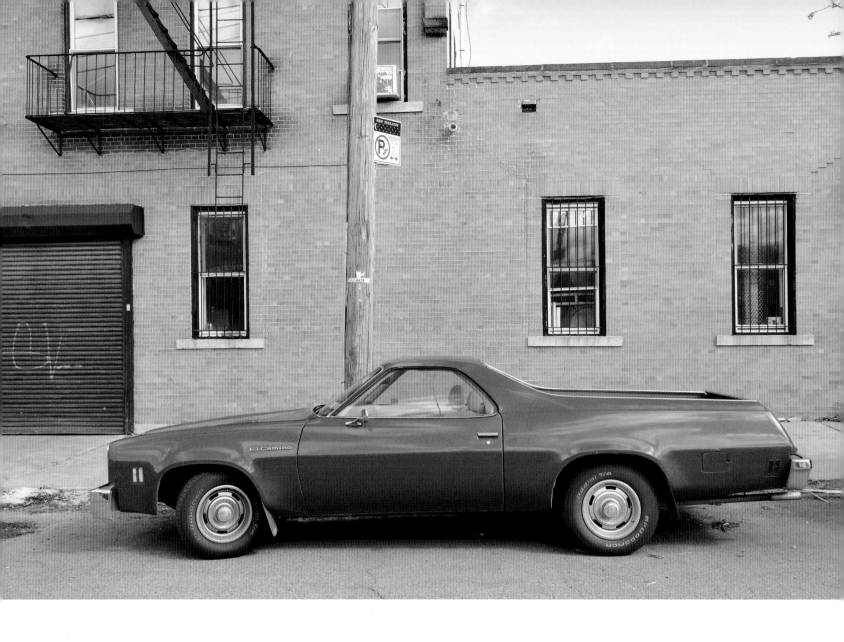

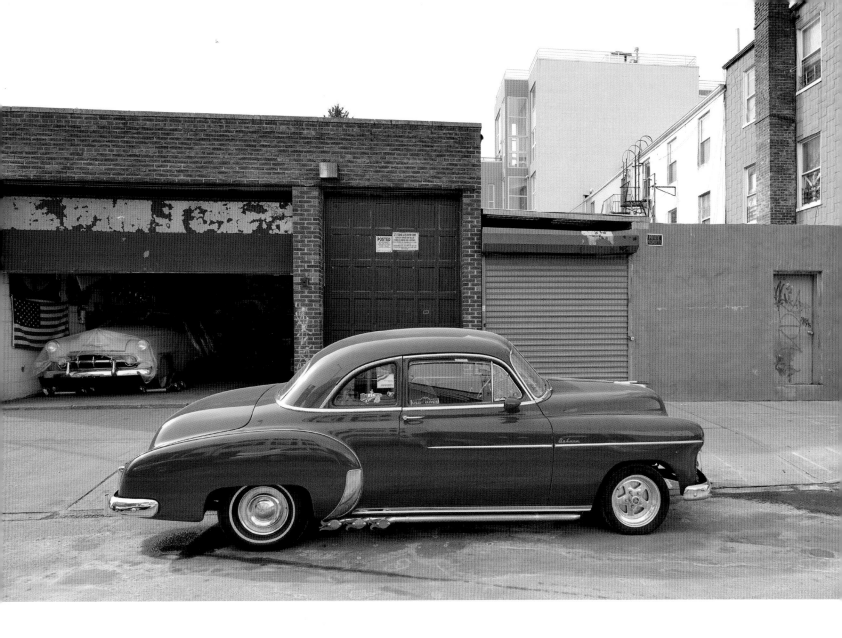

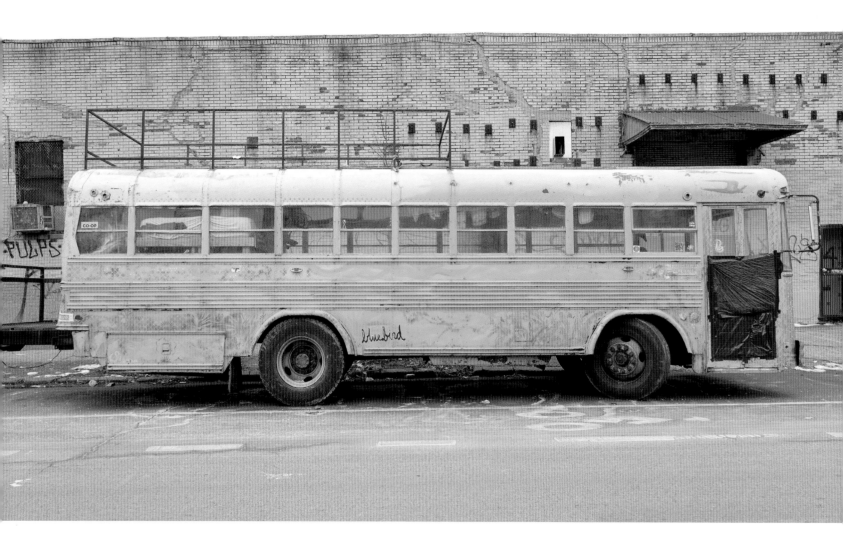

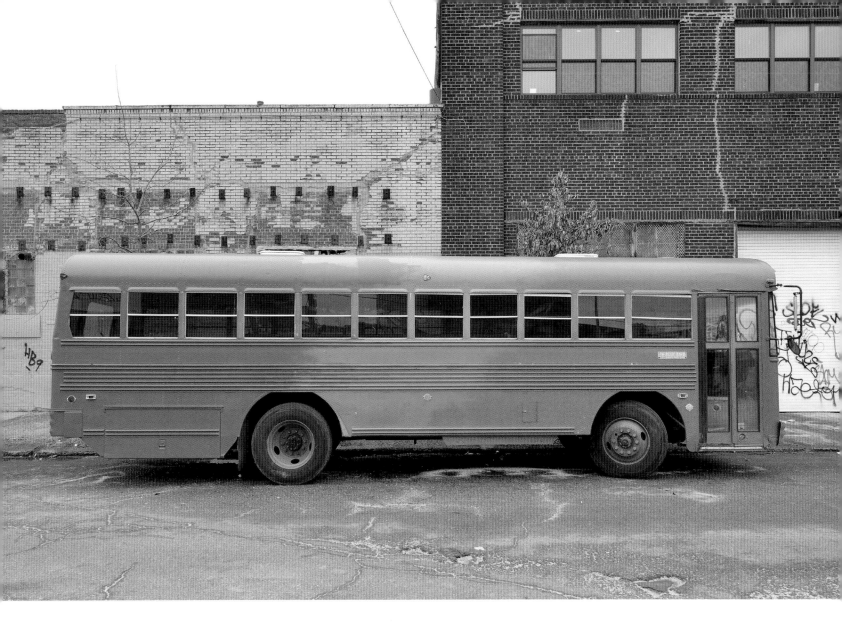

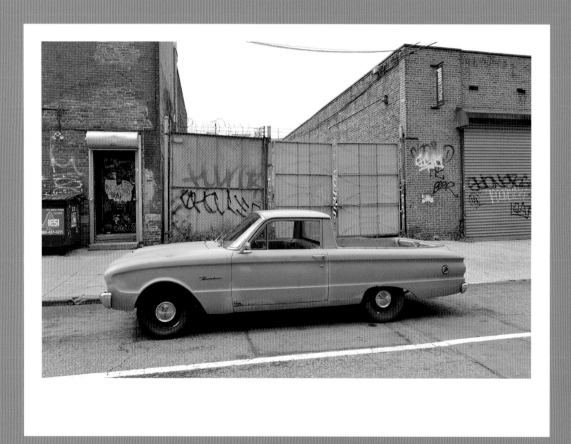

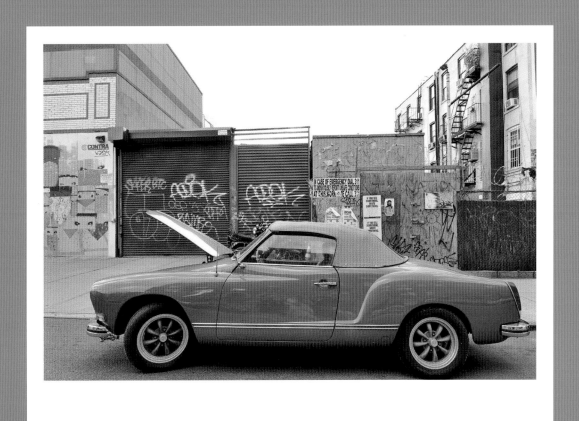

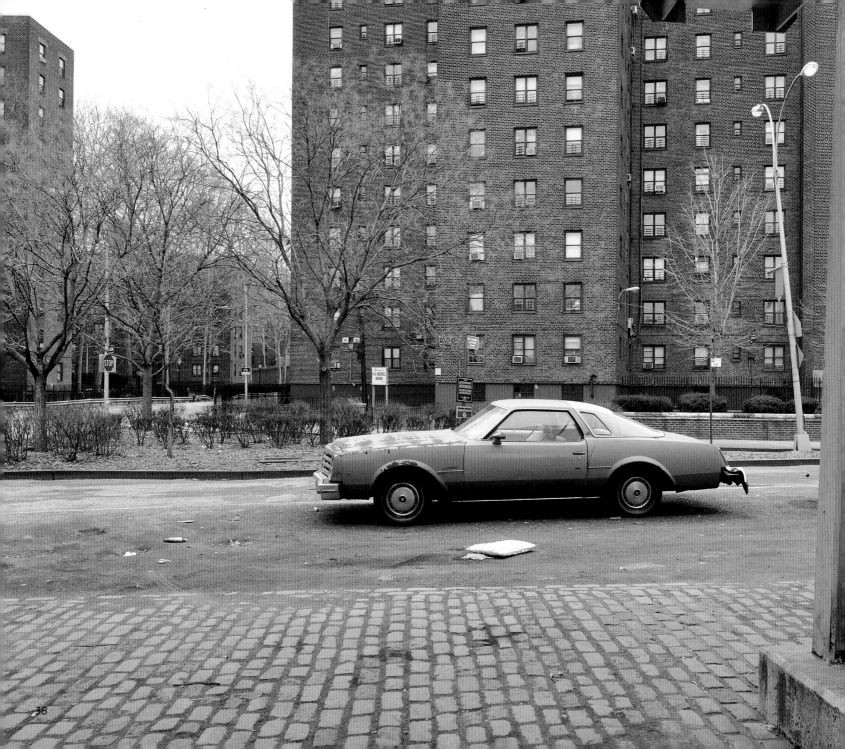

"NO SLEEP 'TIL
BROOKLYN..."

BEASTIE BOYS

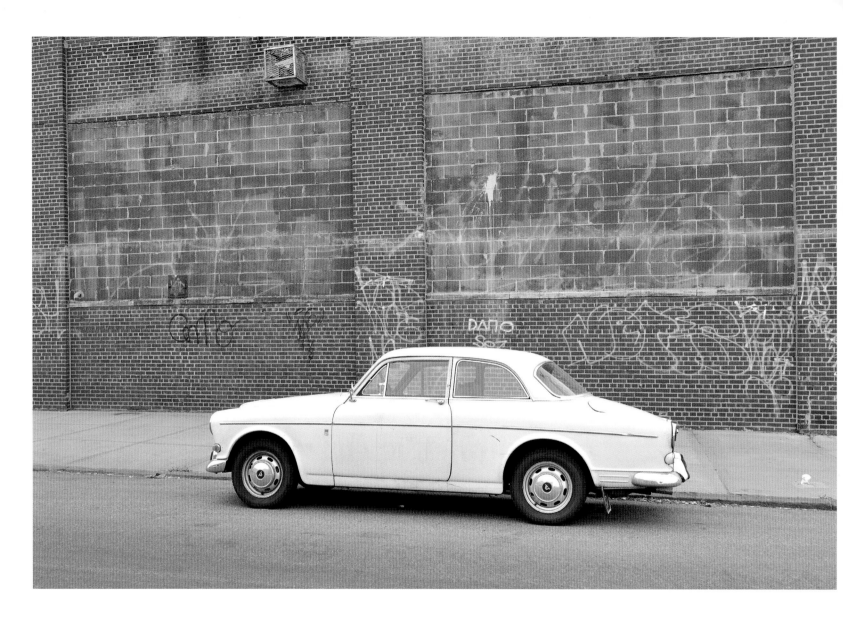

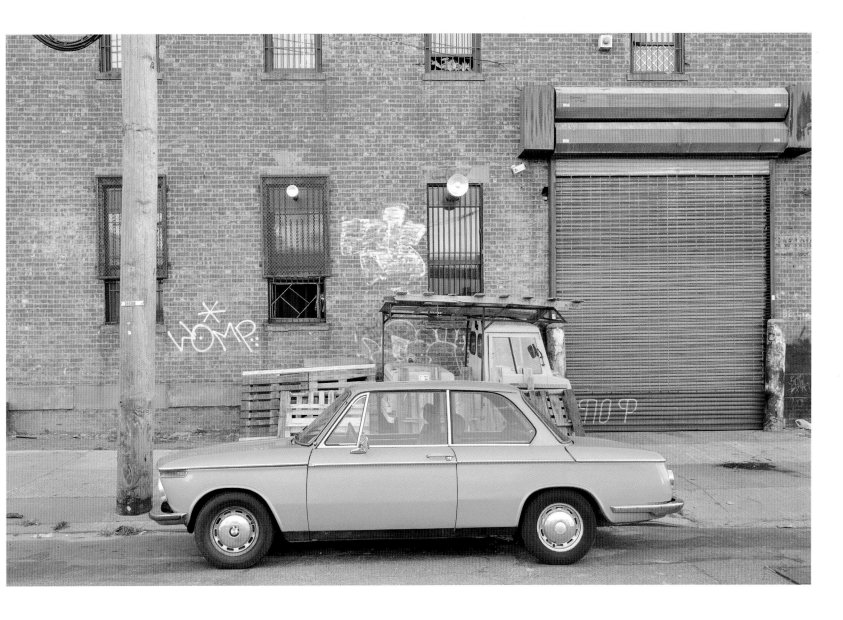

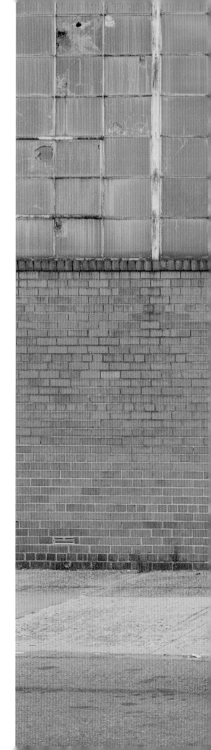

"THE CARS WE DRIVE SAY A LOT ABOUT US."

ENZO FERRARI

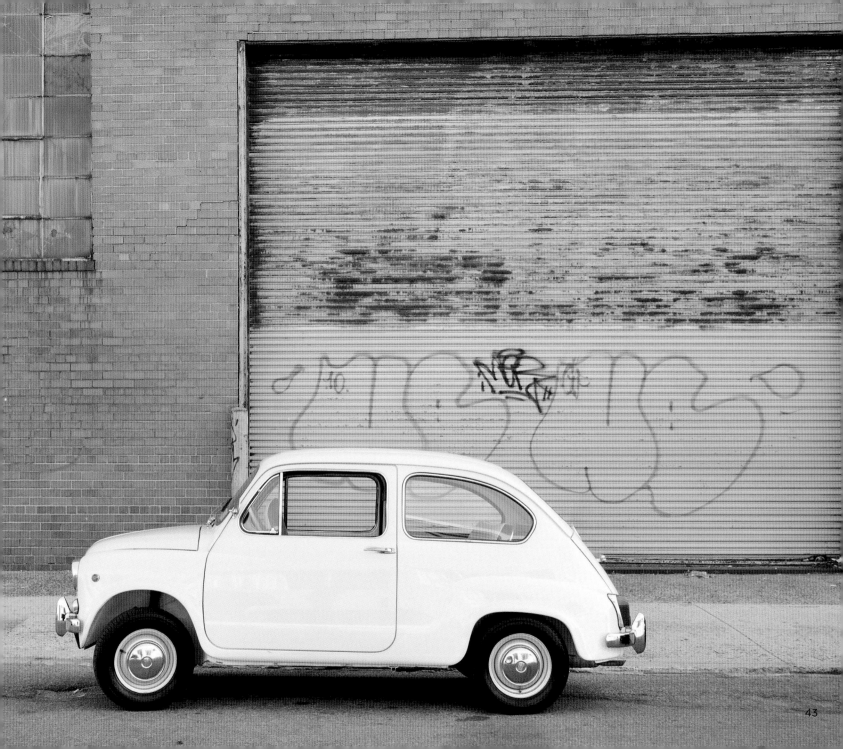

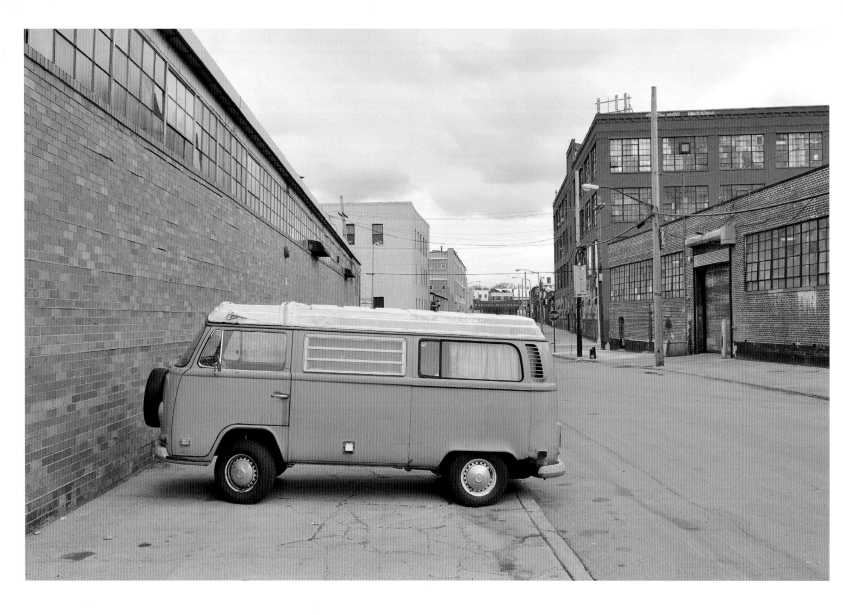

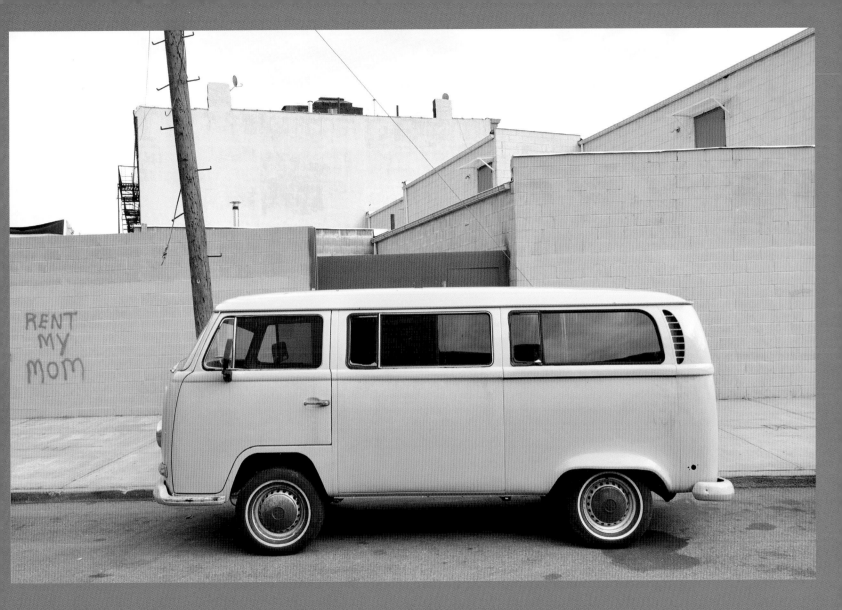

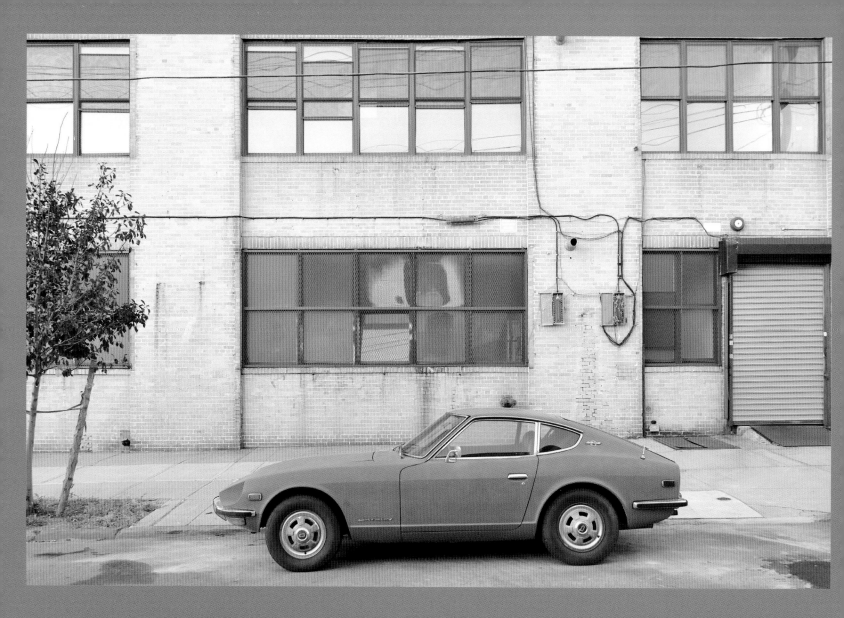

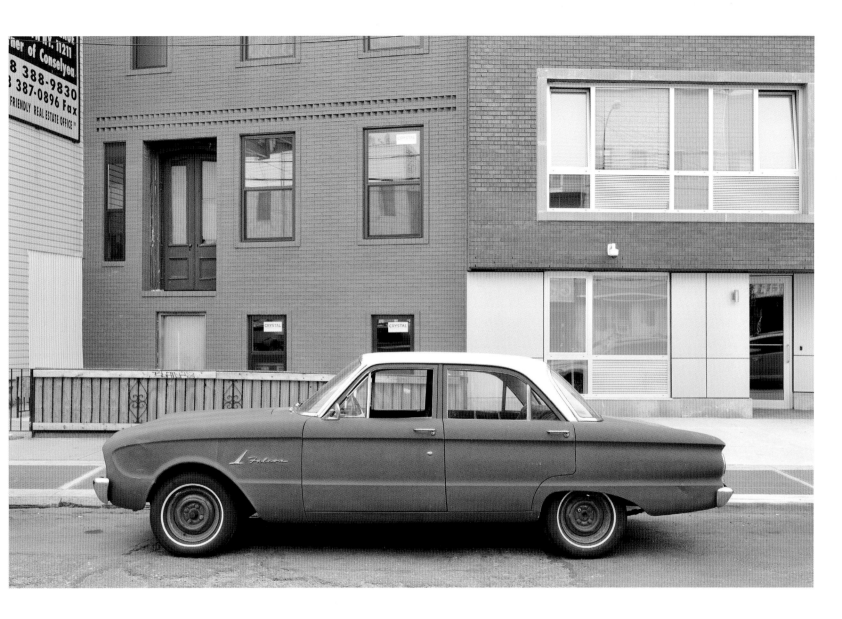

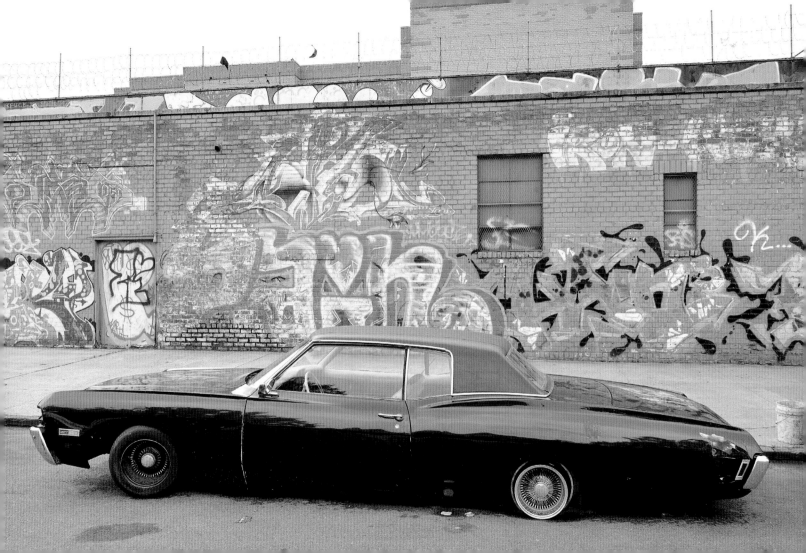

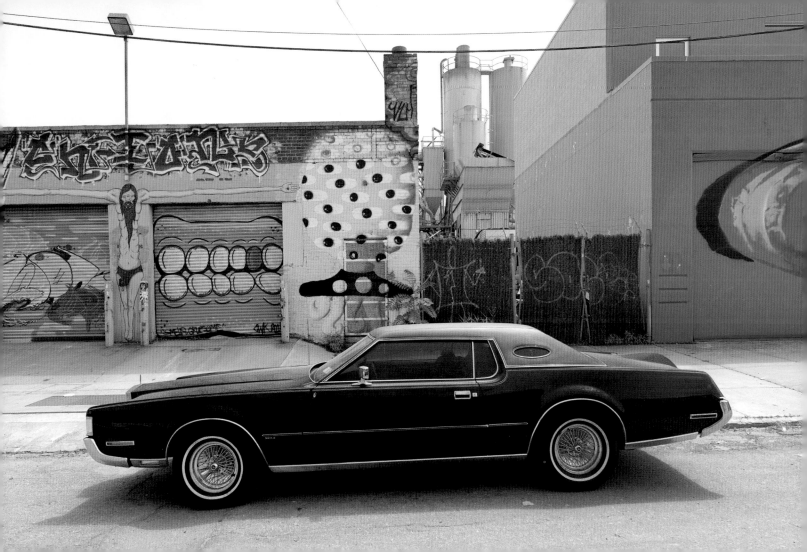

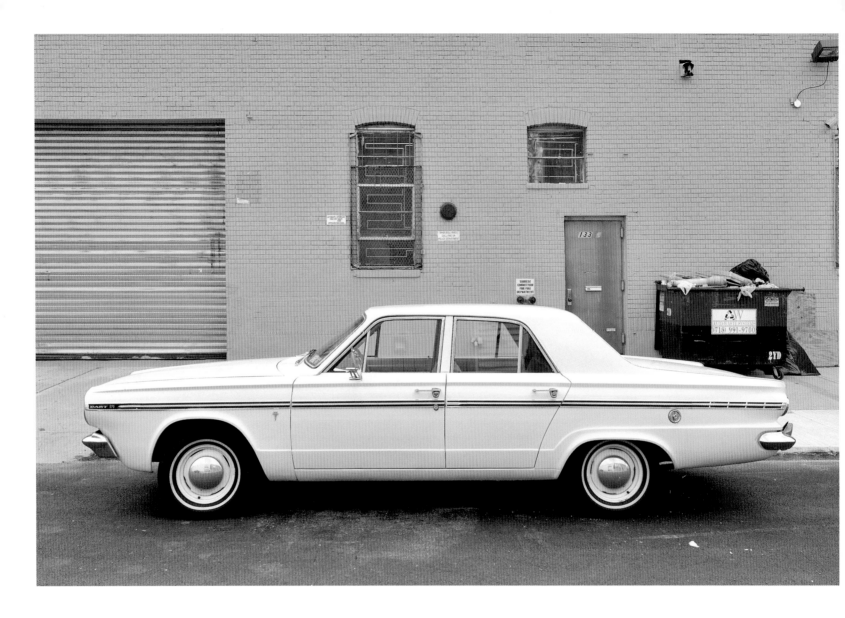

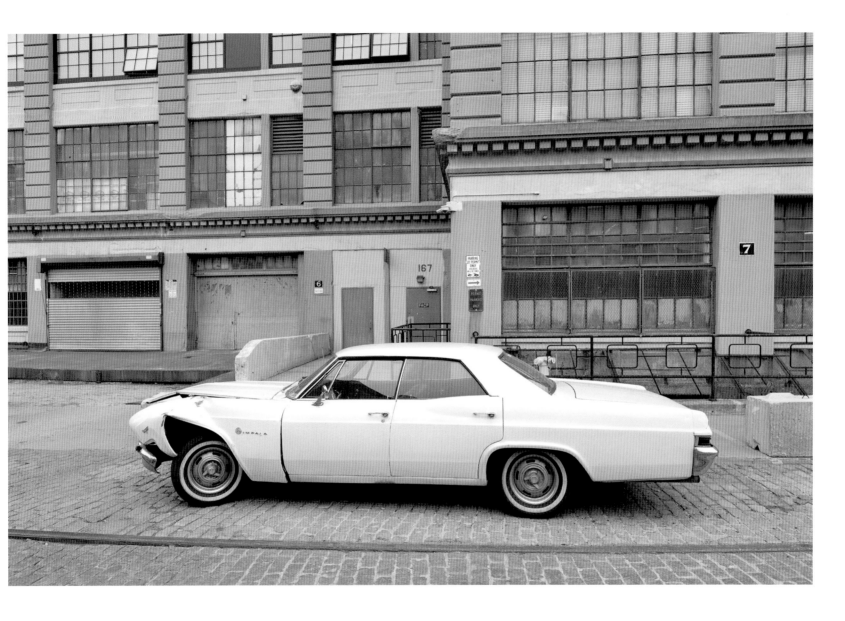

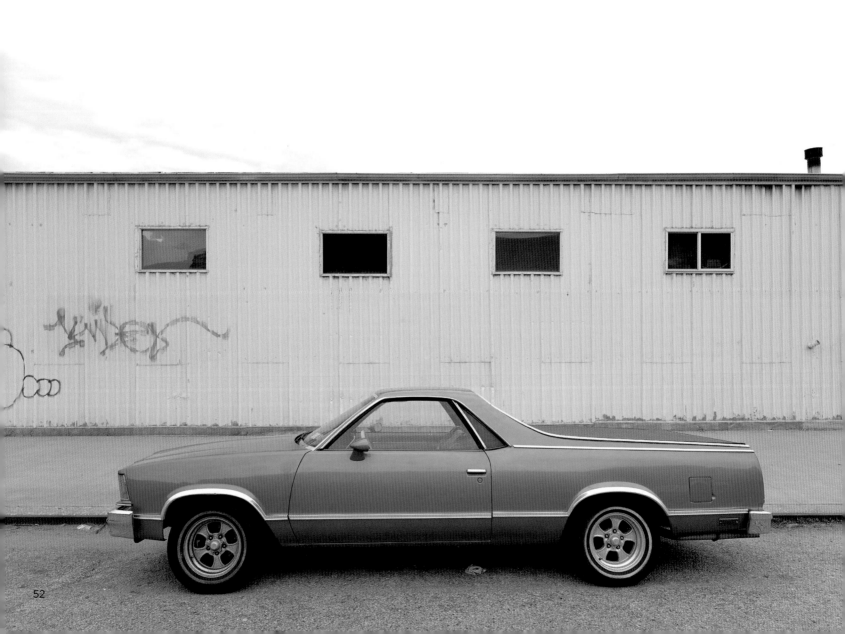

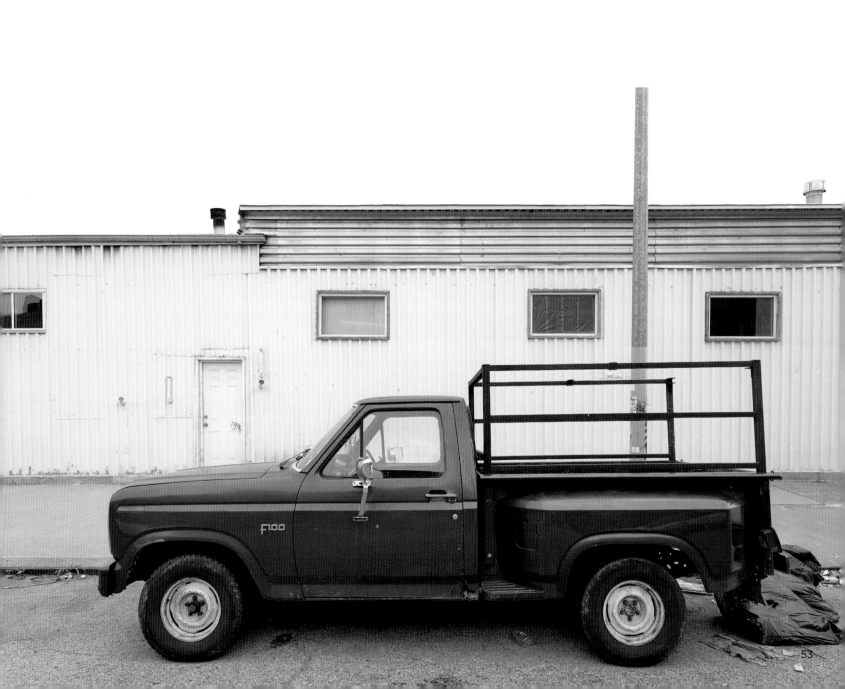

53

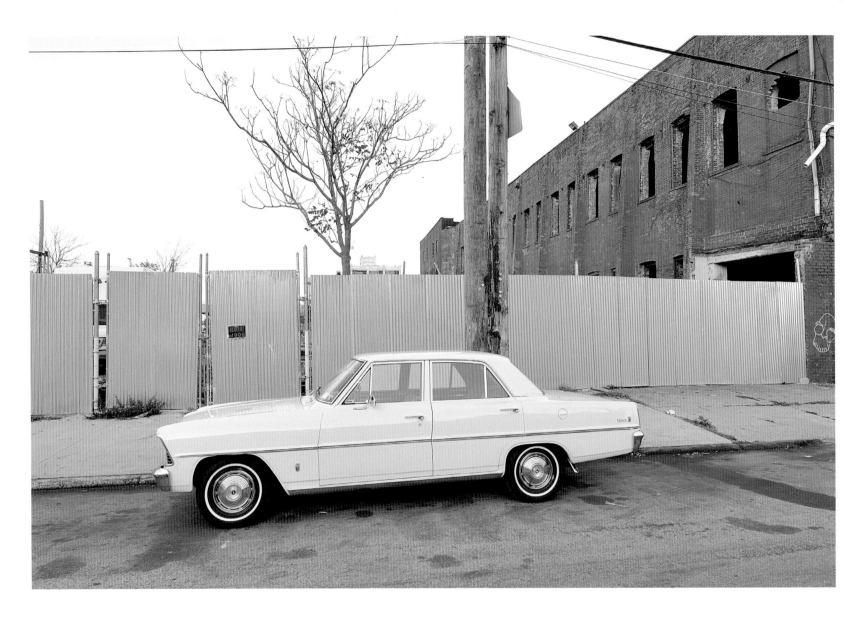

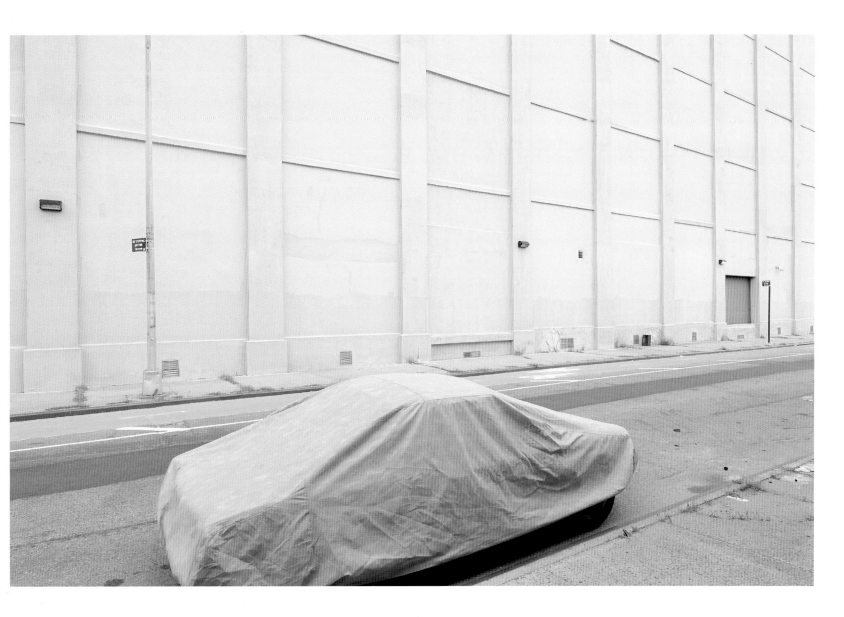

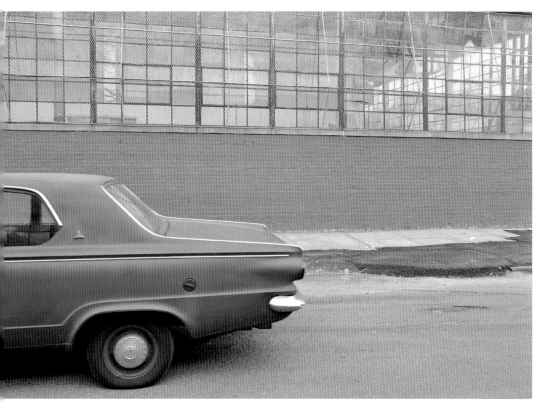
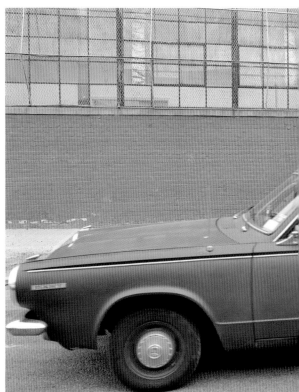

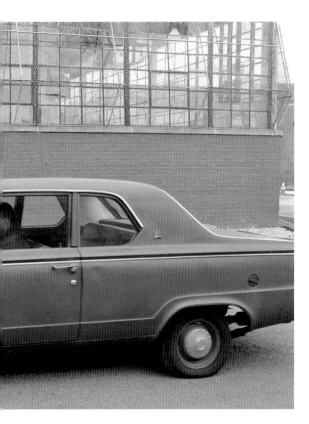
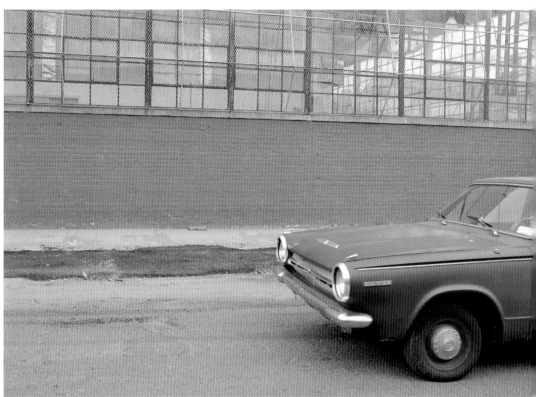

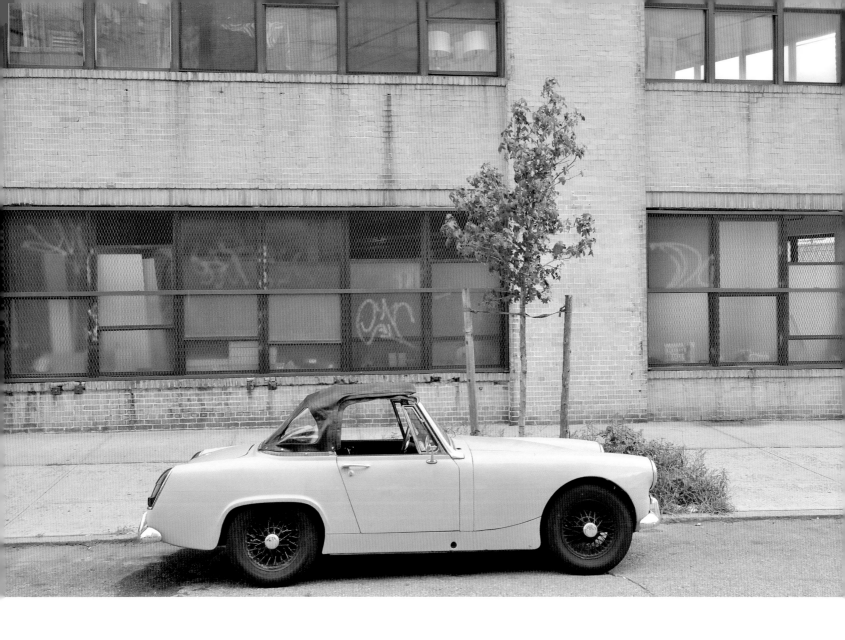

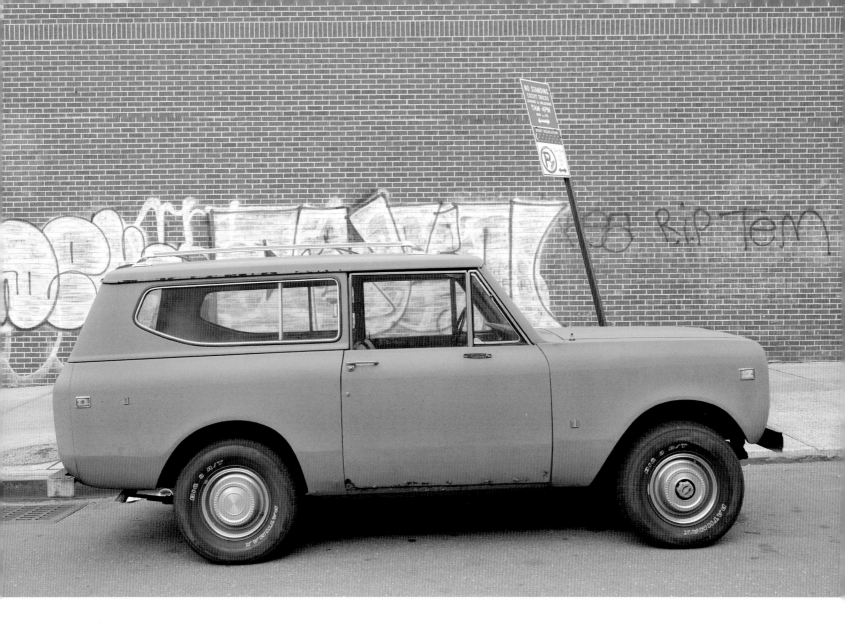

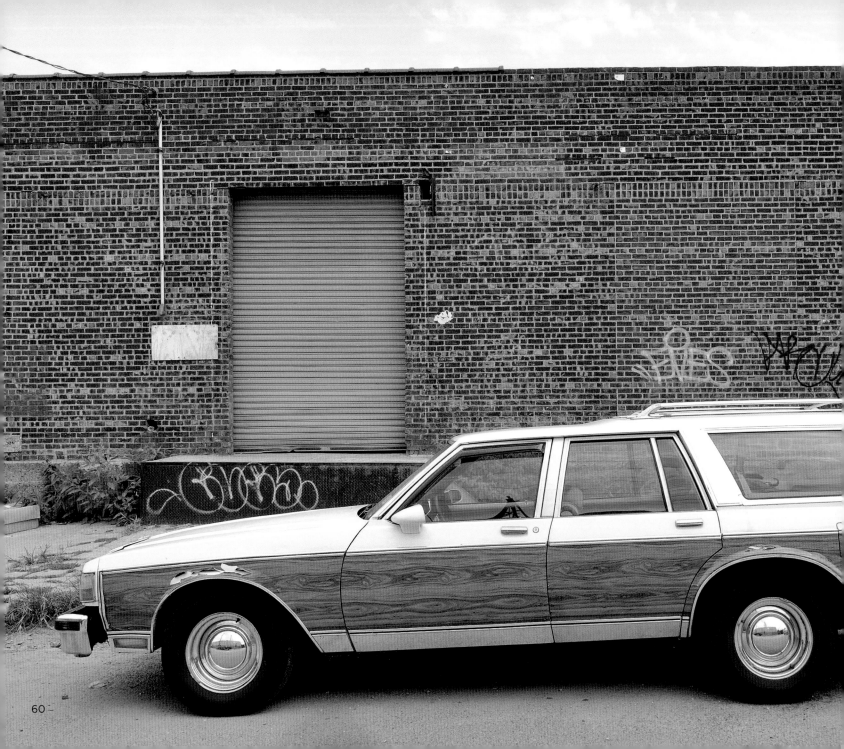

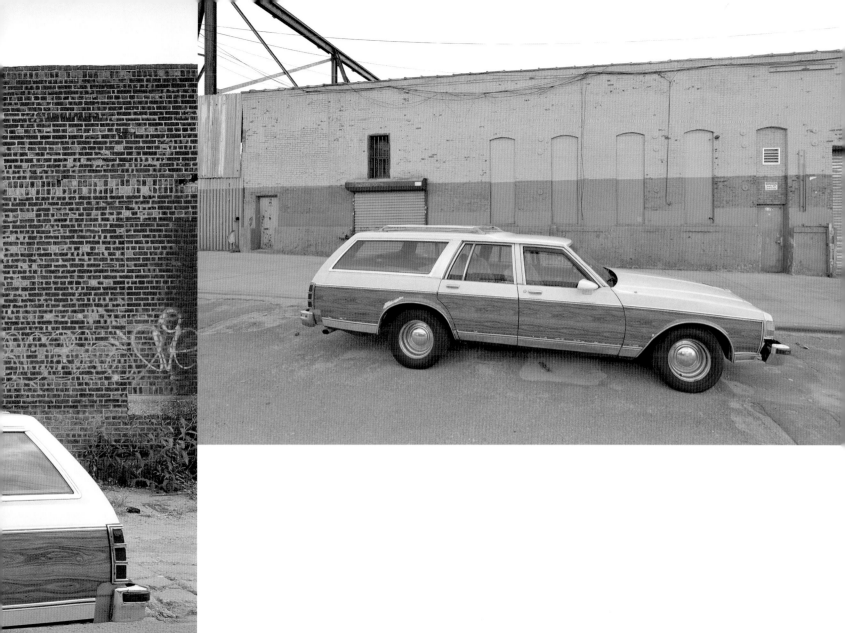

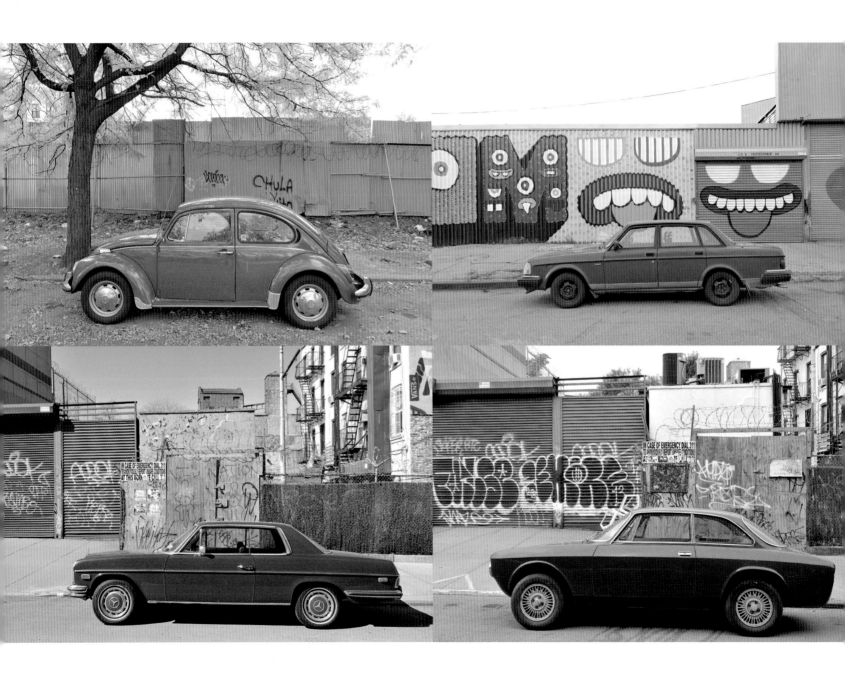

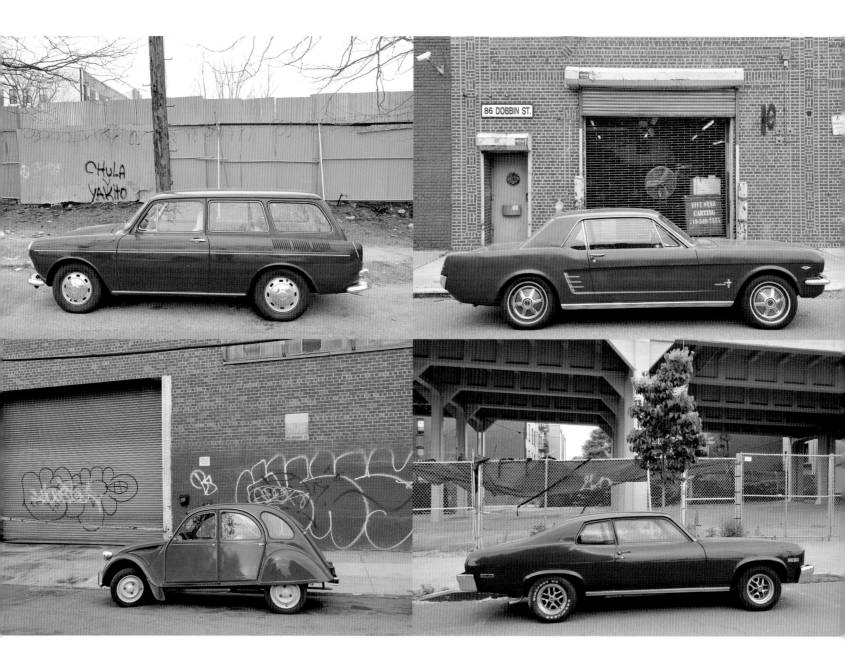

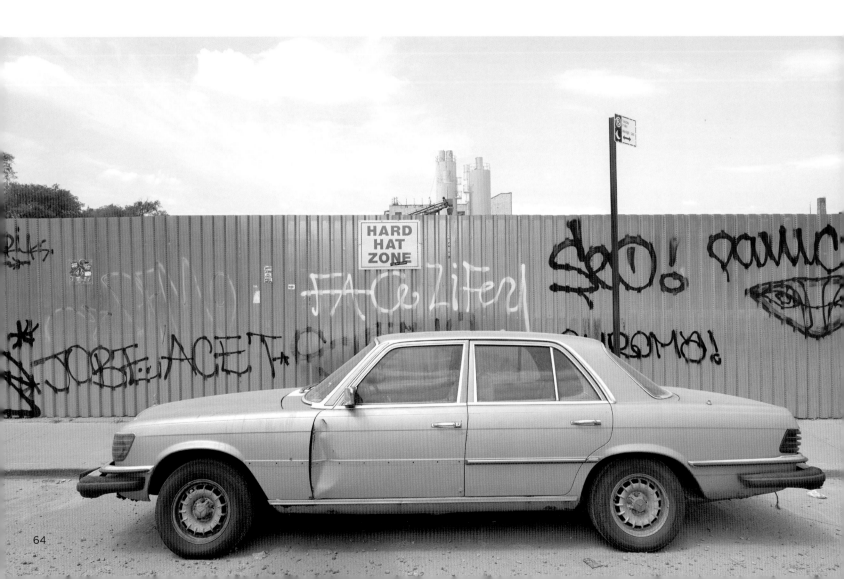

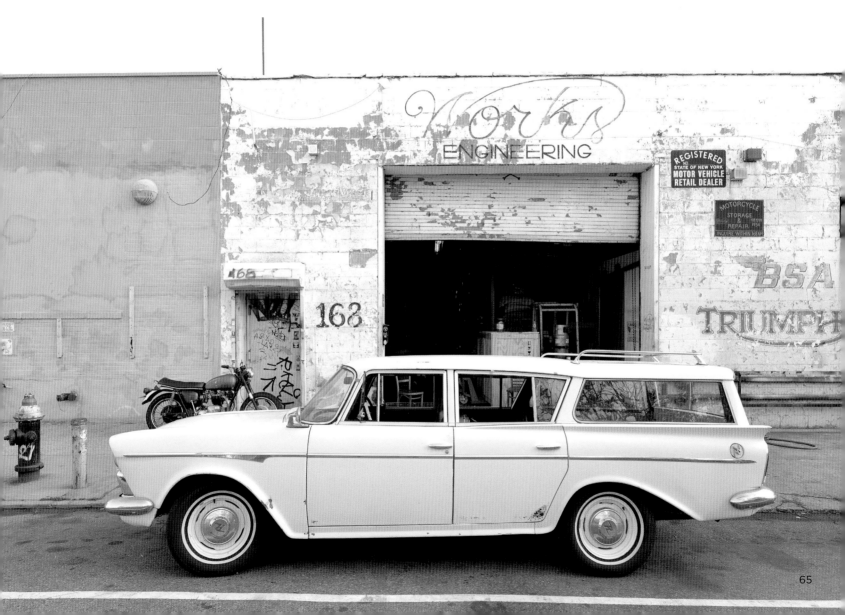

"EVERYTHING
IN LIFE IS
SOMEWHERE
ELSE, AND YOU
GET THERE
IN A CAR."

E.B. WHITE

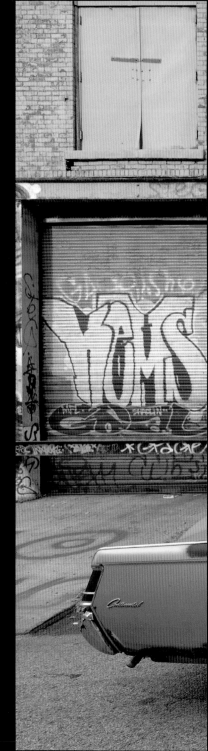

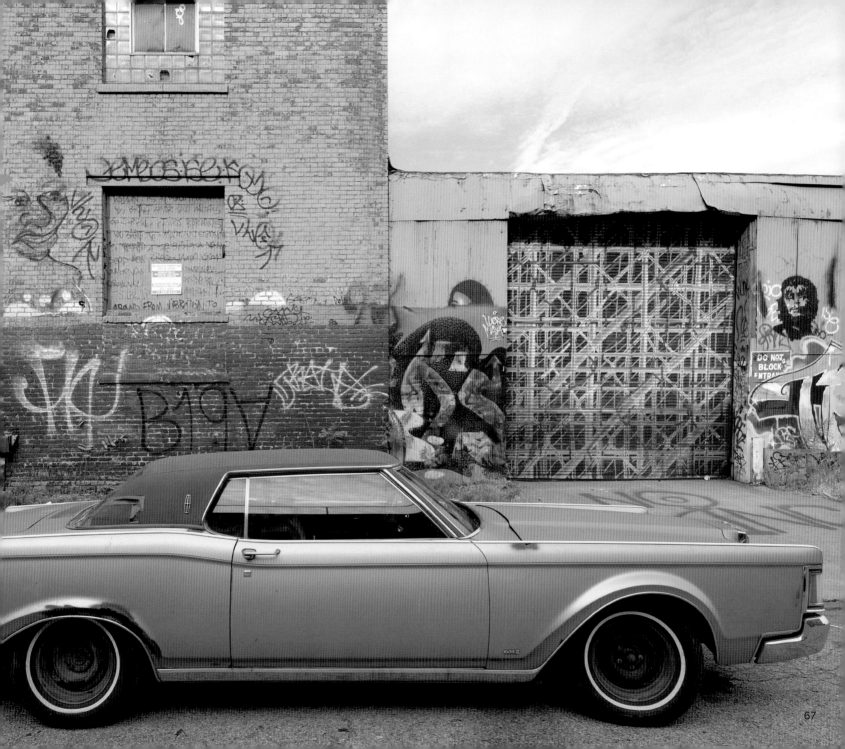

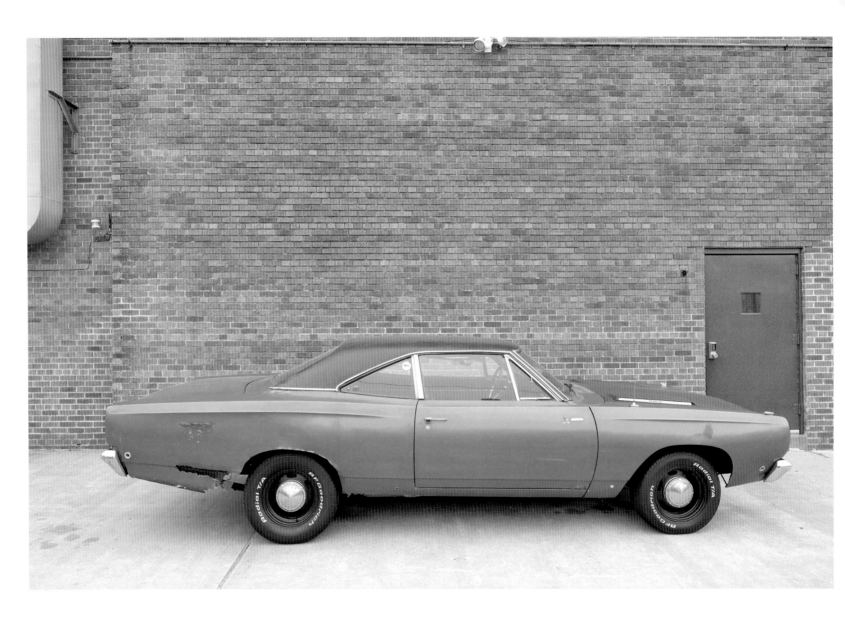

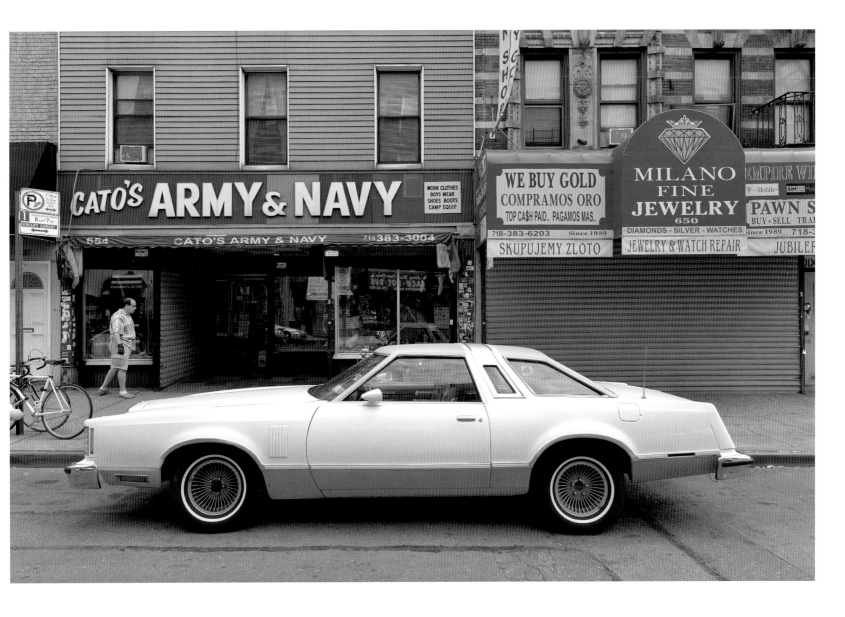

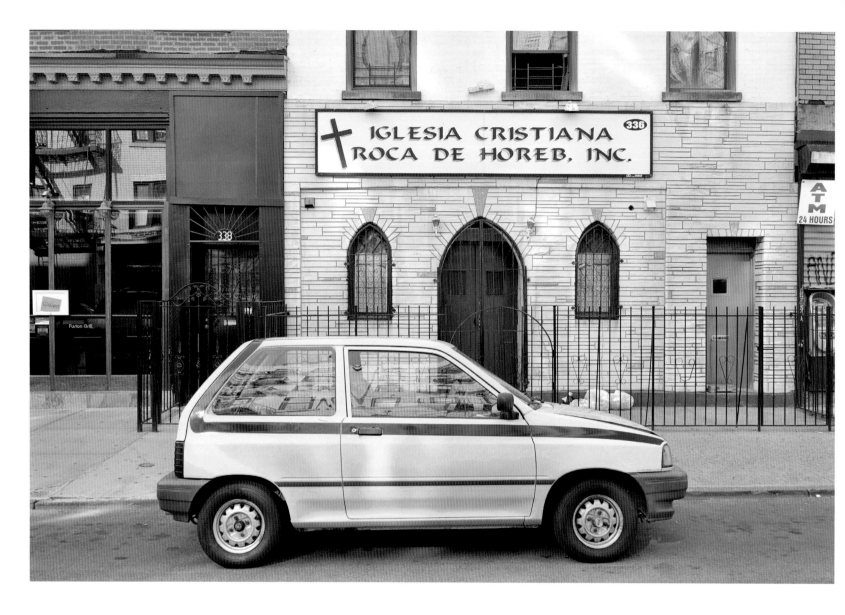

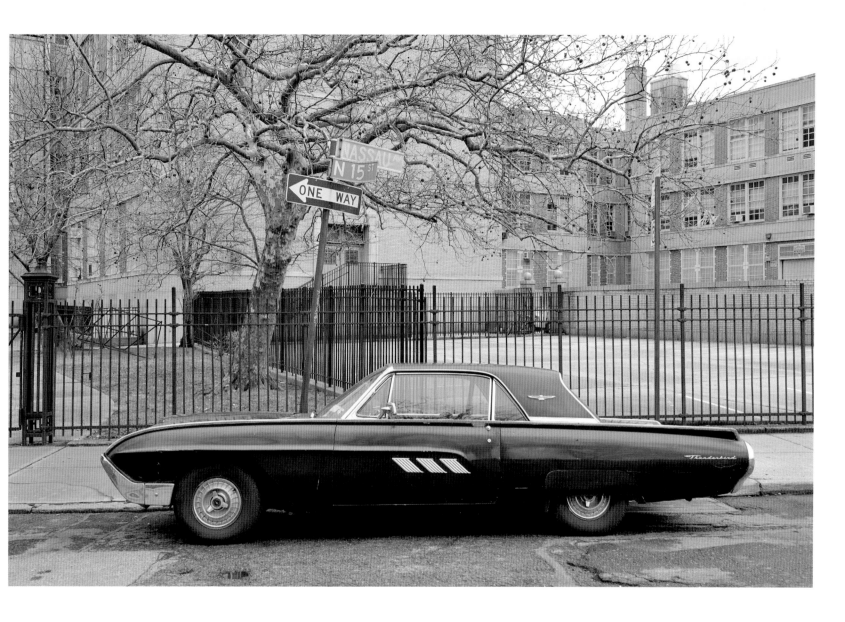

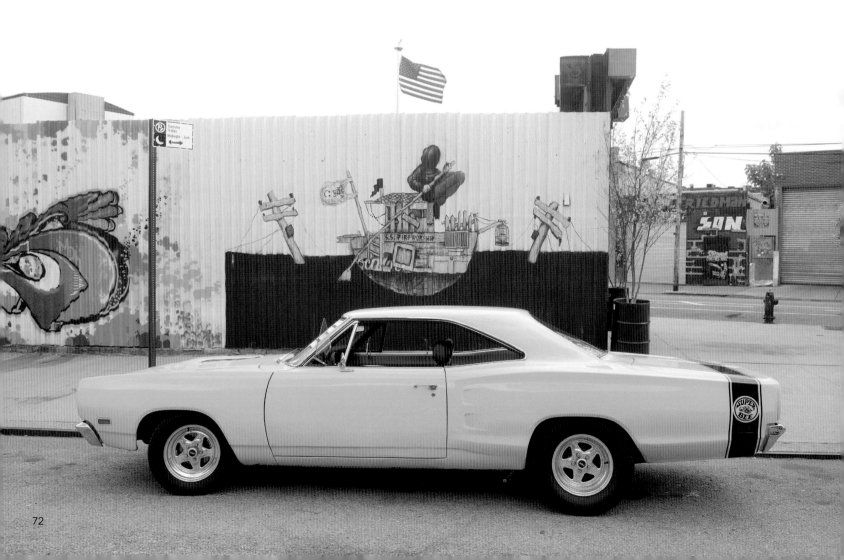

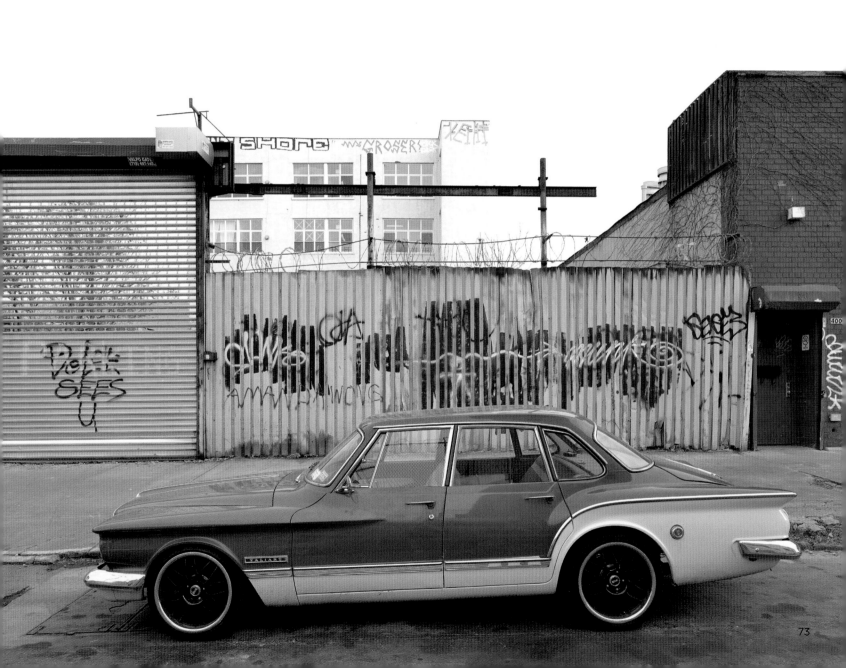

"I BEEN A LONG
TIME LEAVING
BUT I'M GOING
TO BE A LONG
TIME GONE."

WILLIE NELSON

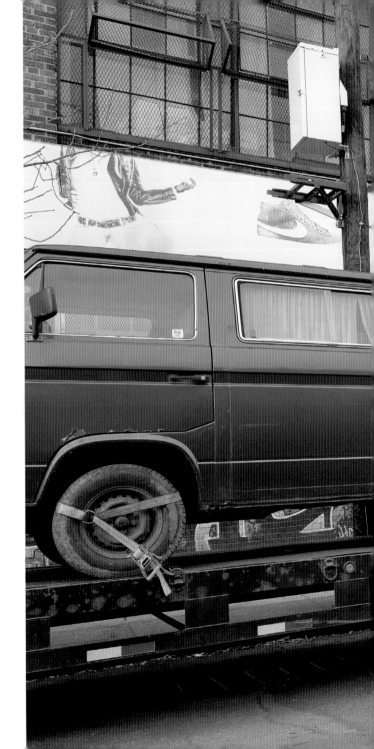

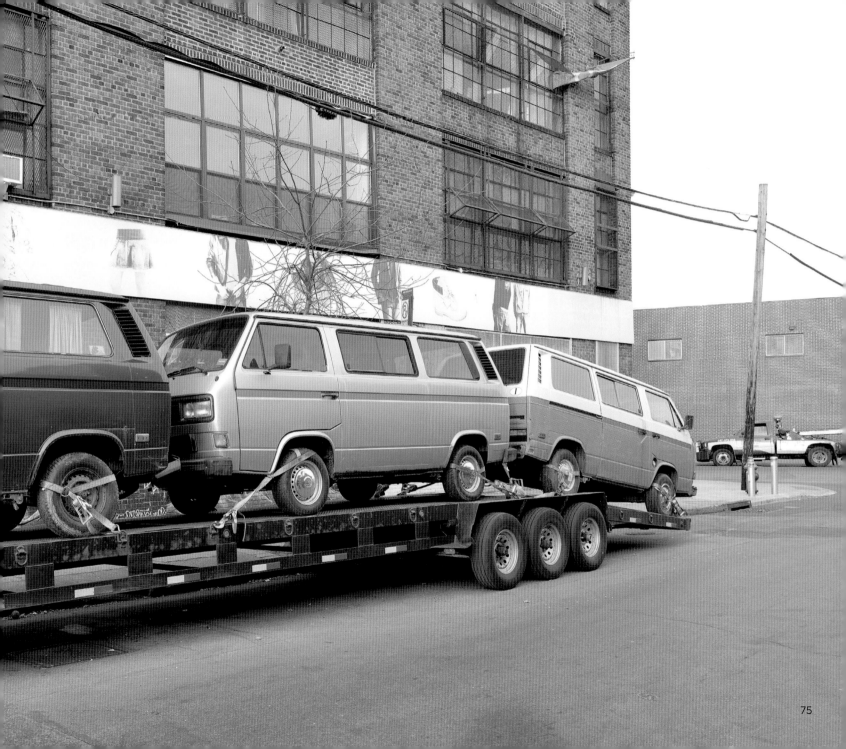

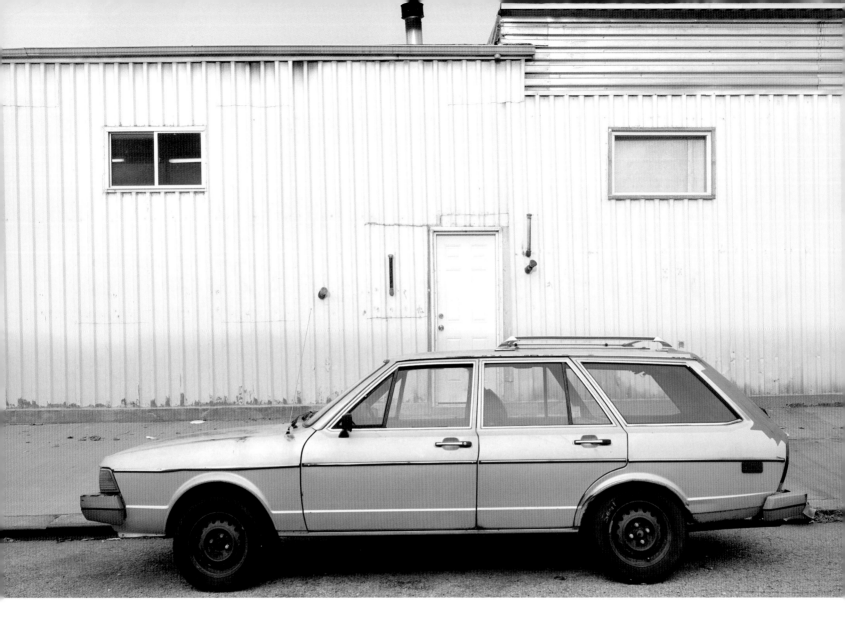

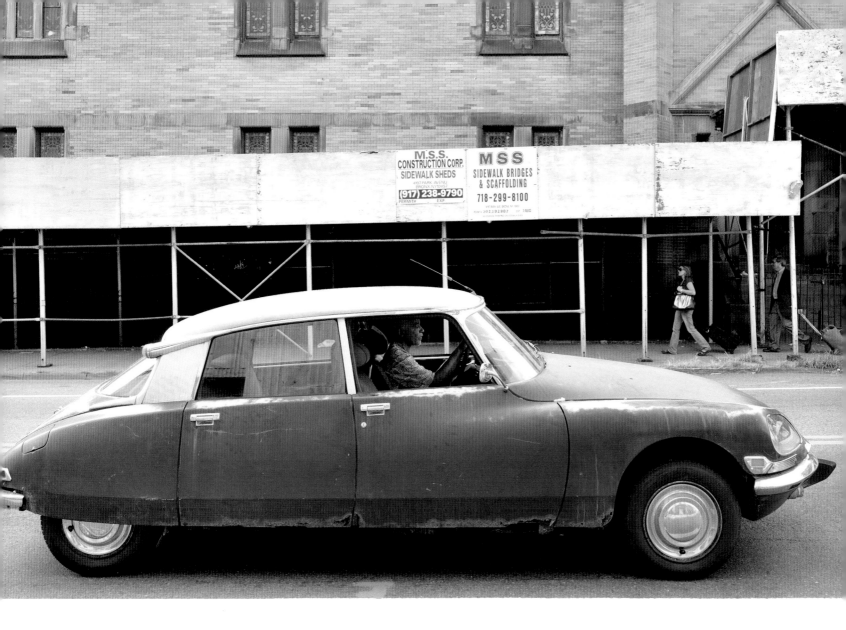

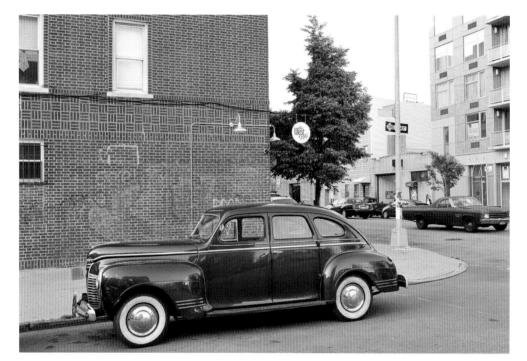

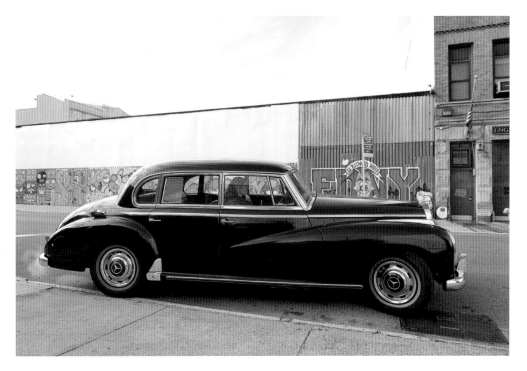

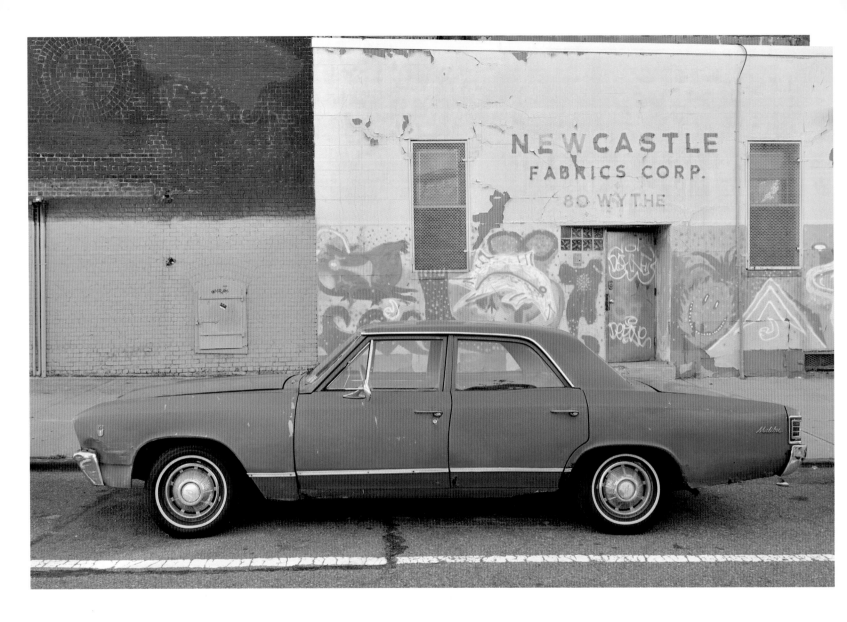

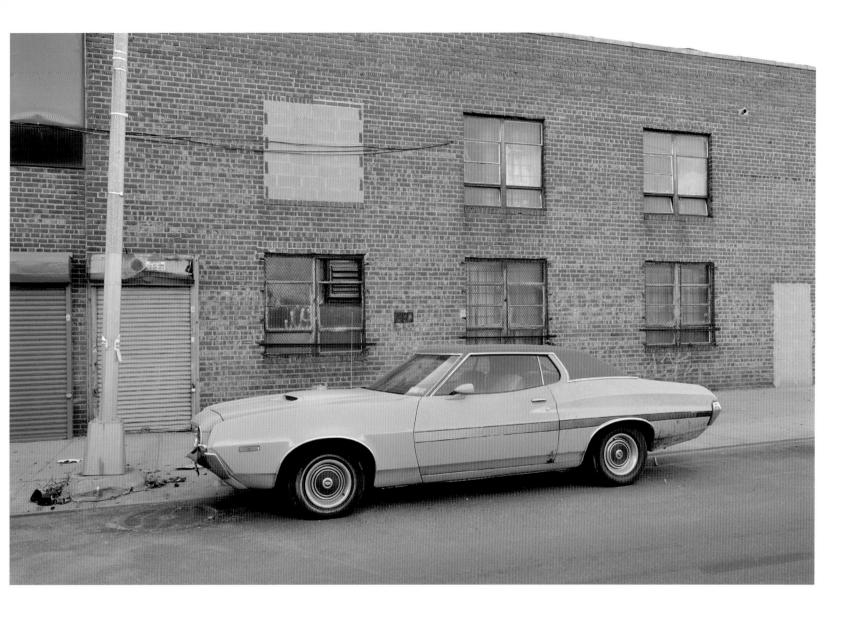

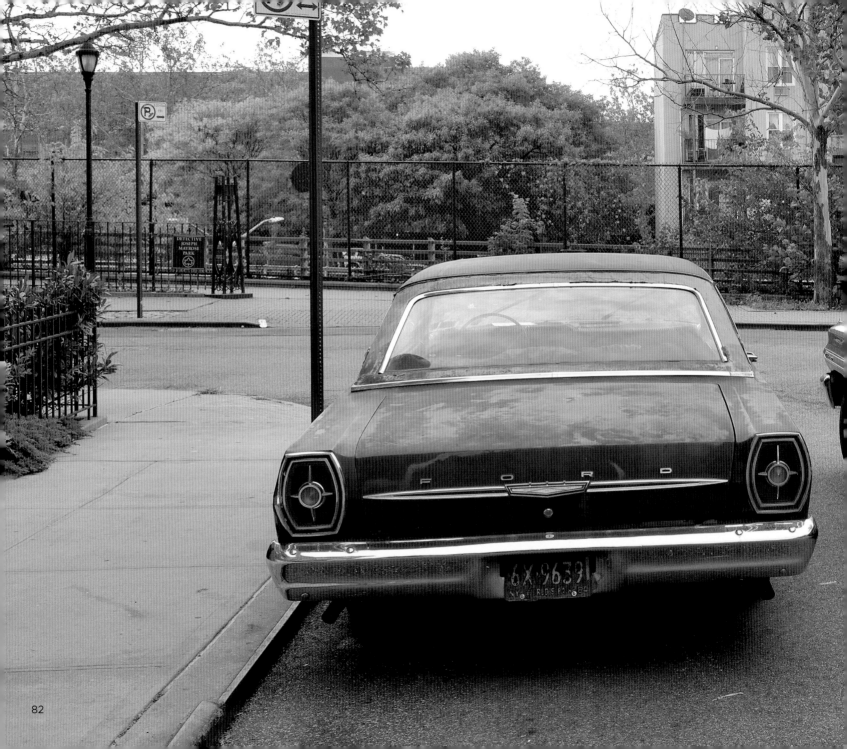

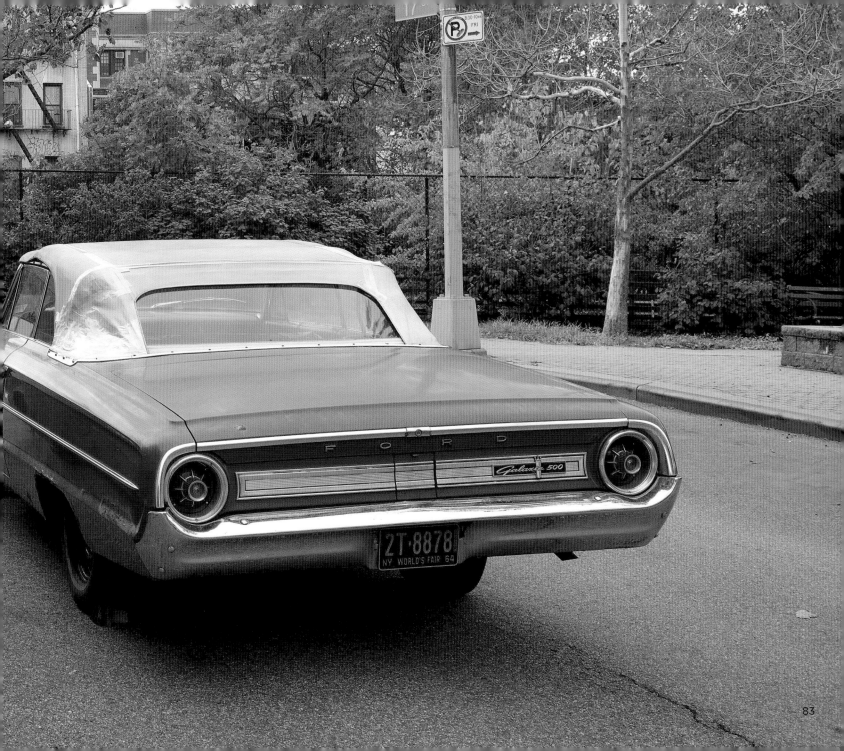

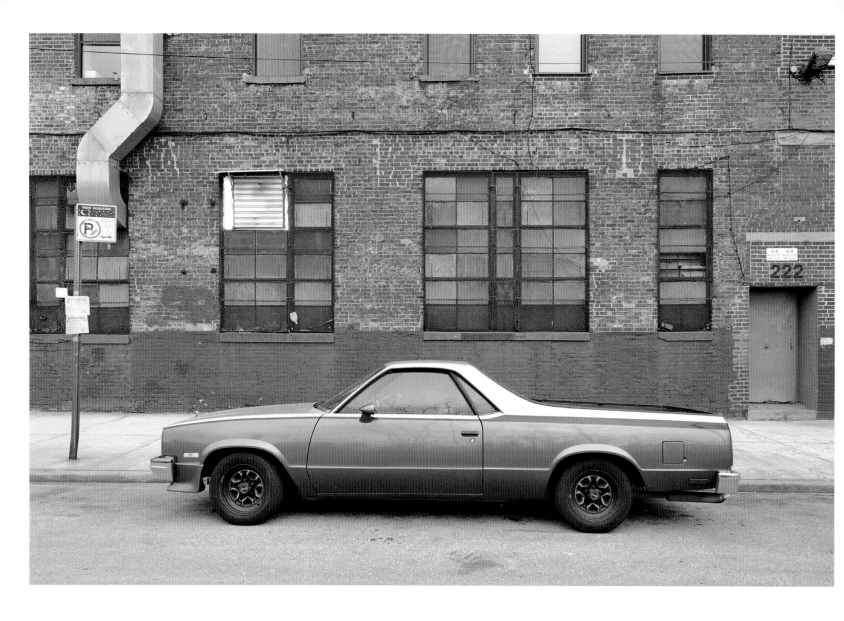

84

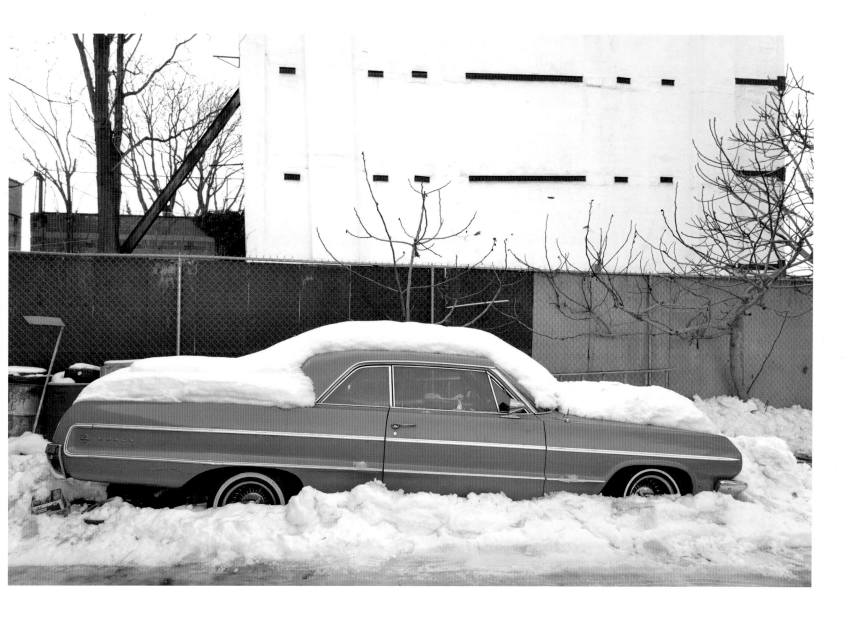

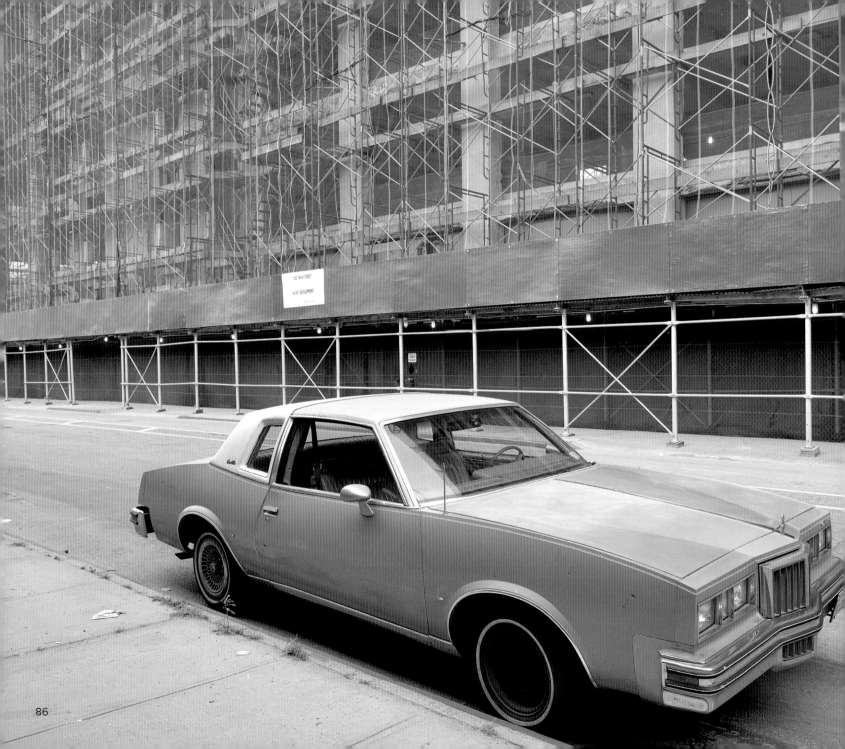

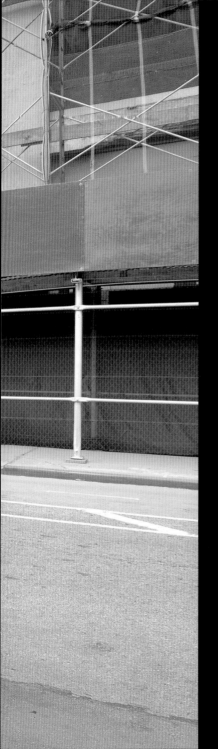

"MY BIGG
IN LIFE I
FORGOT

EVA PERON

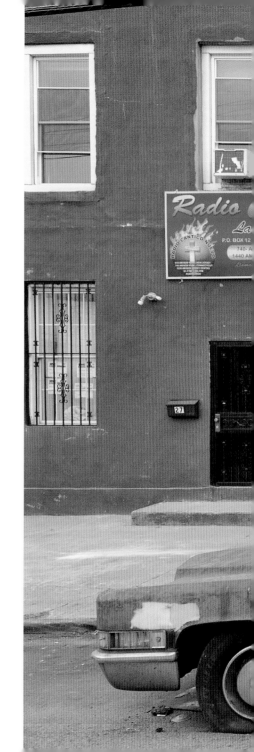

"CARS ARE THE
SCULPTURES OF
OUR EVERYDAY
LIVES."

CHRIS BANGLE

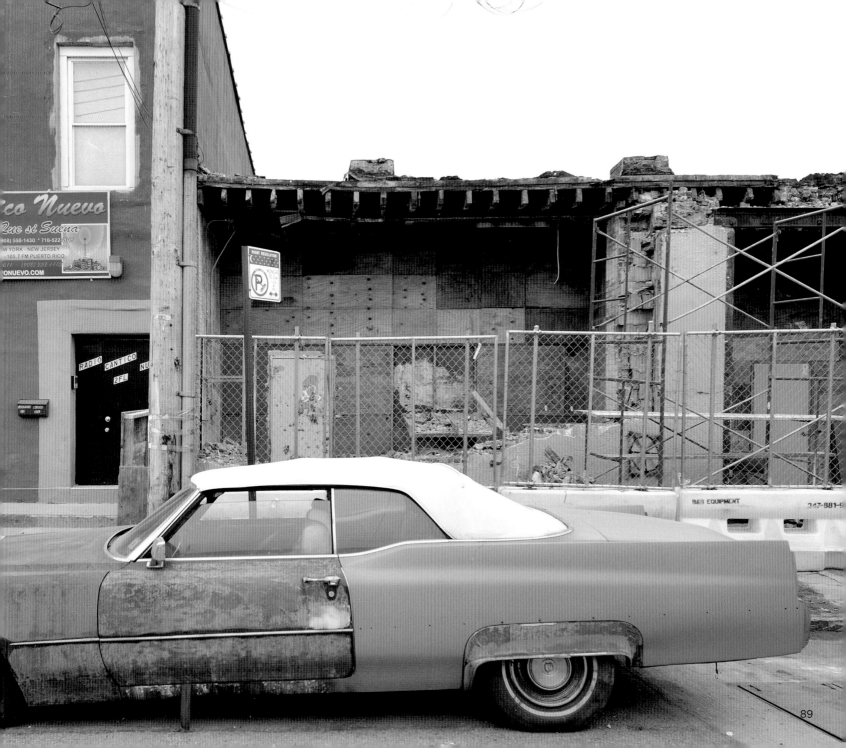

89

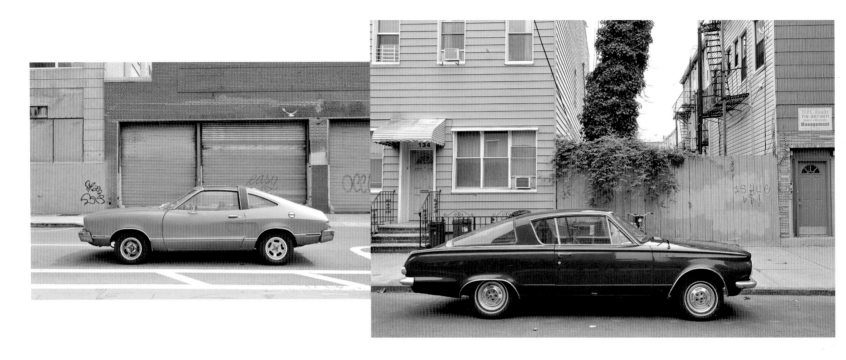

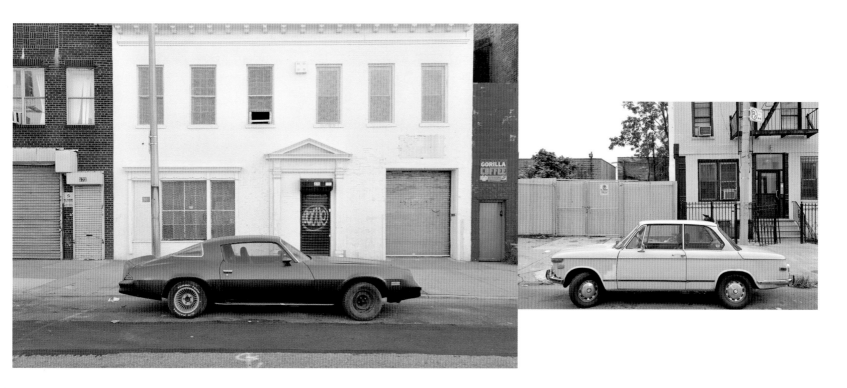

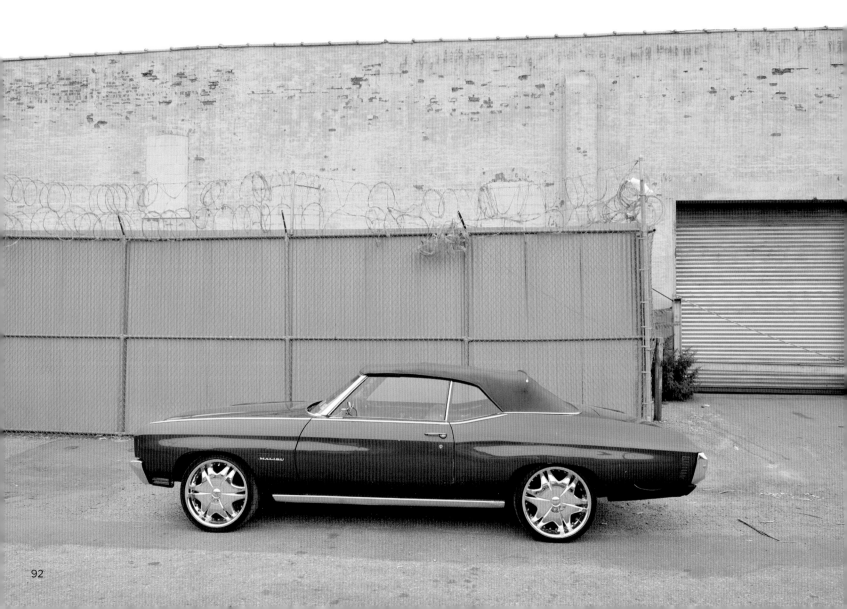

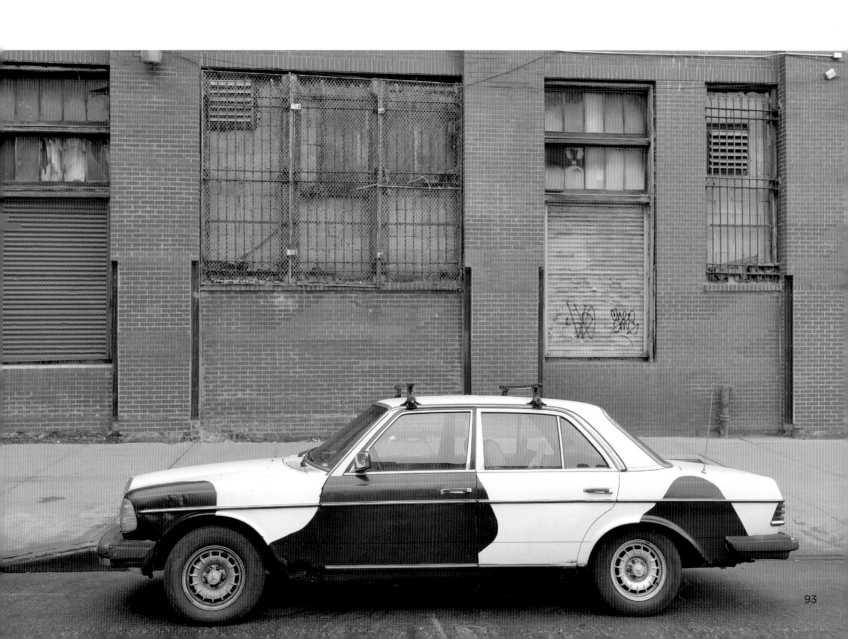

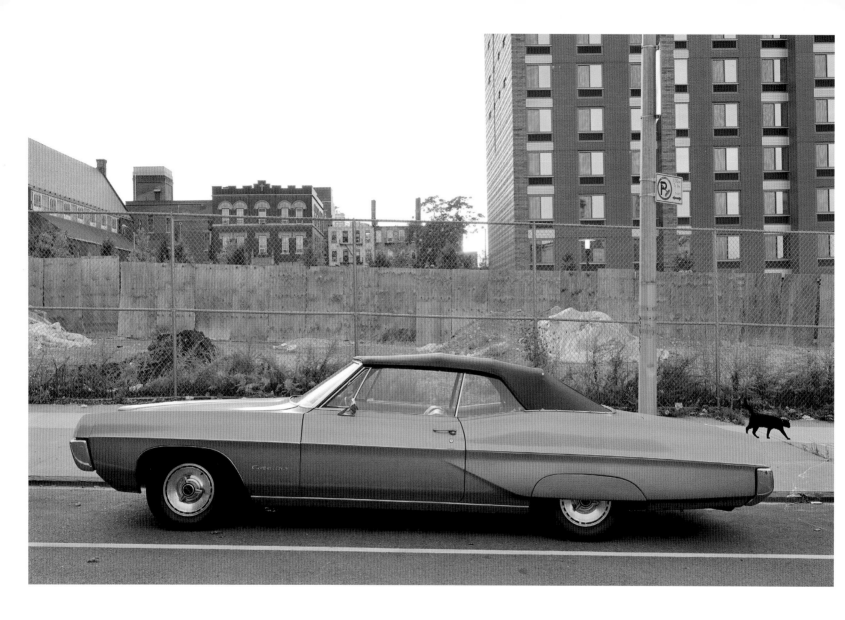

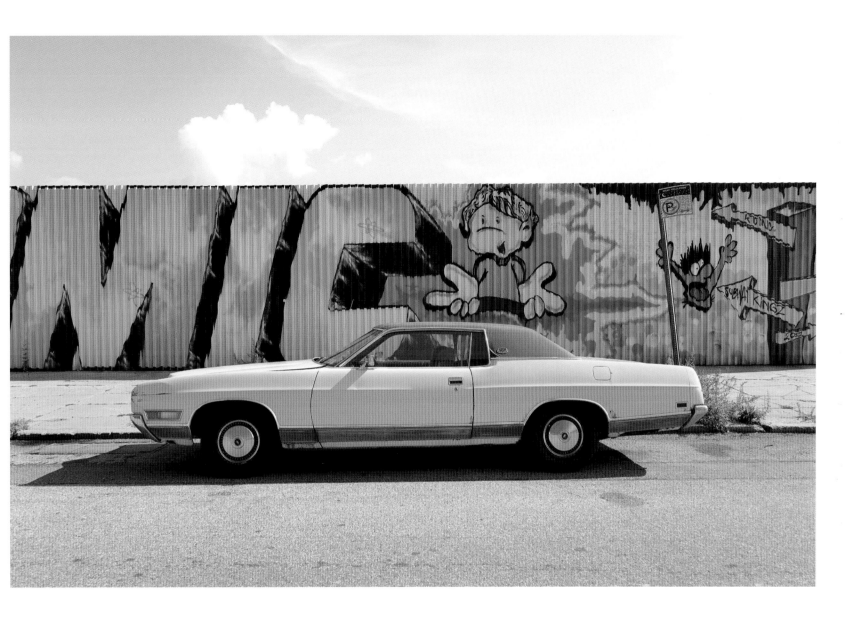

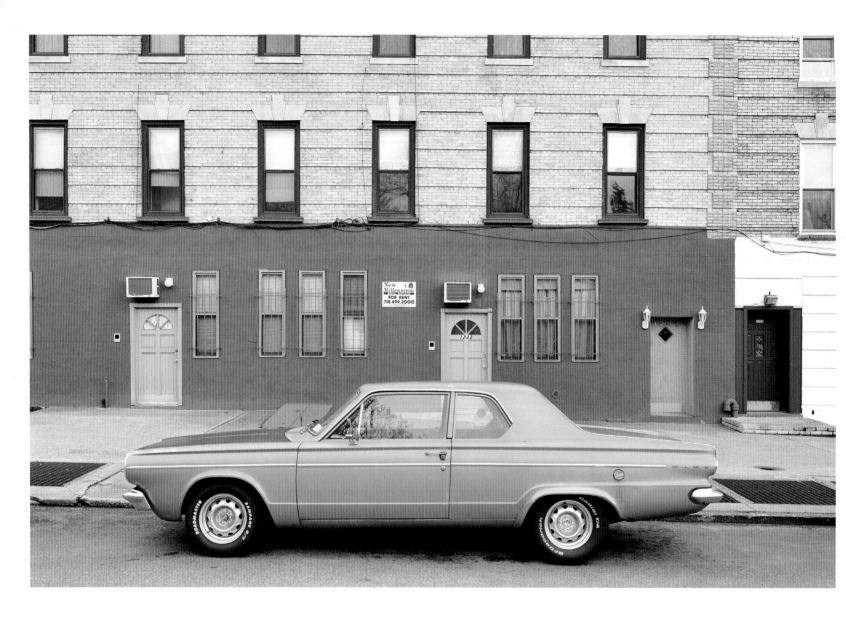

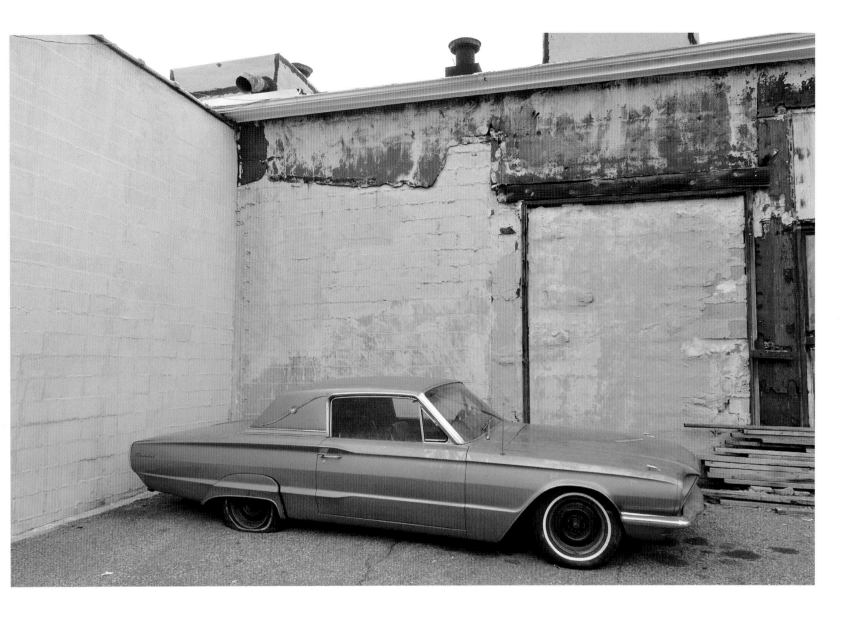

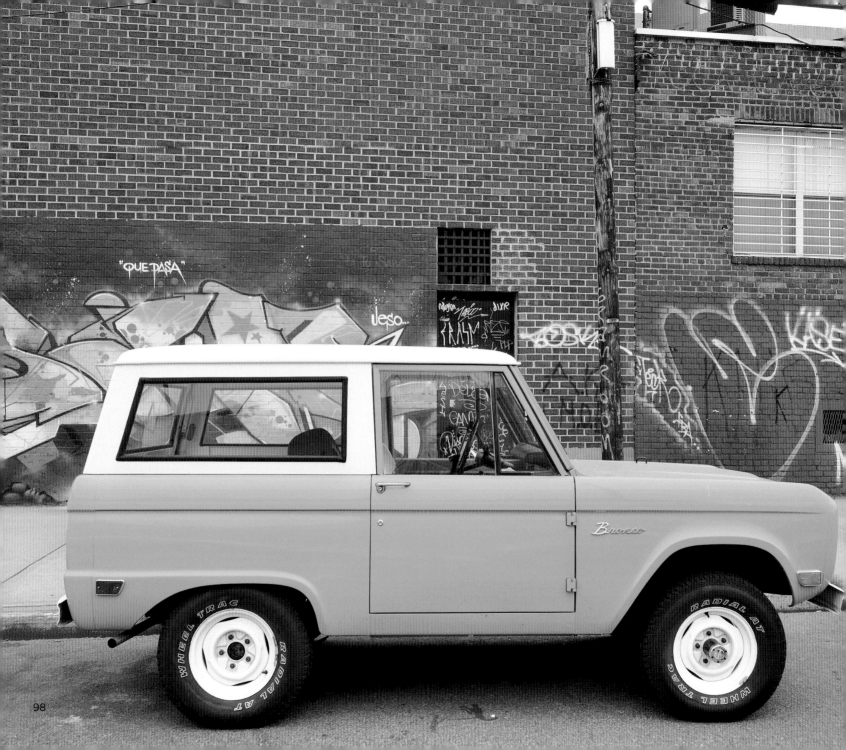

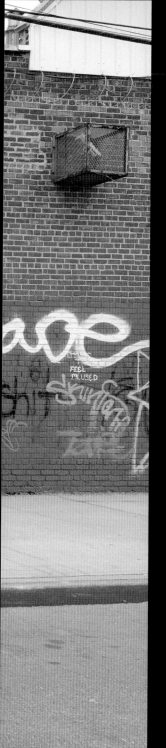

"WHEN I DIE, BURY ME IN MY JEEP. THERE'S NEVER BEEN A HOLE IT COULDN GET OUT OF."

SOURCE UNKNOWN

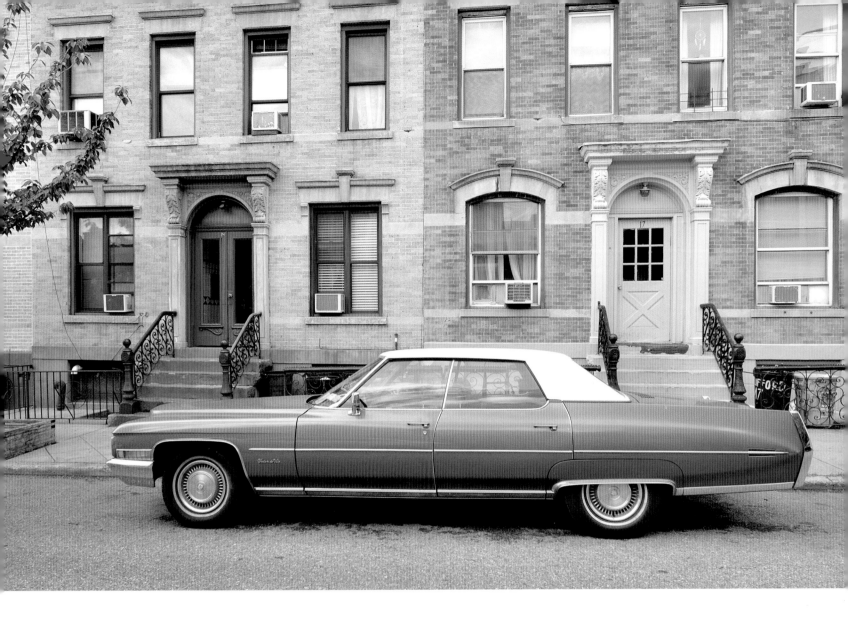

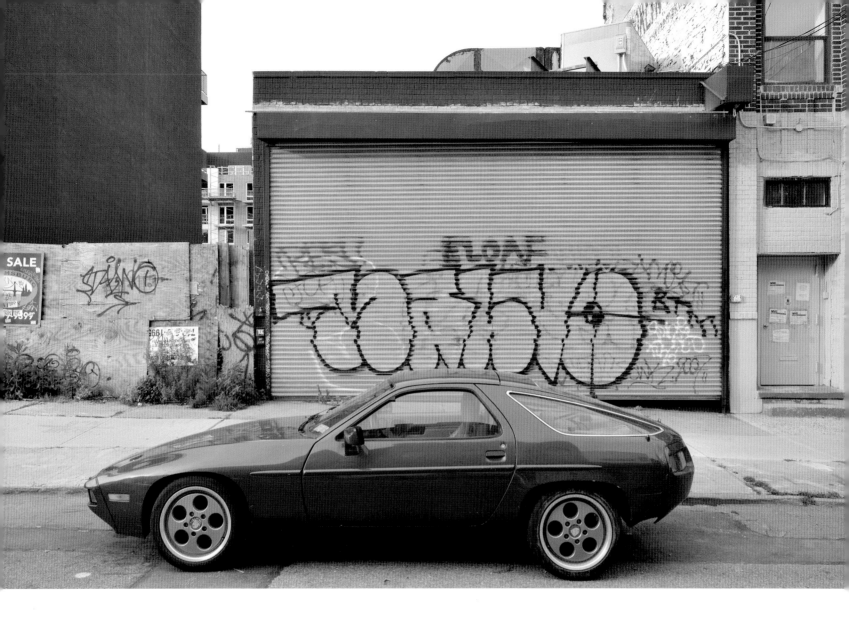

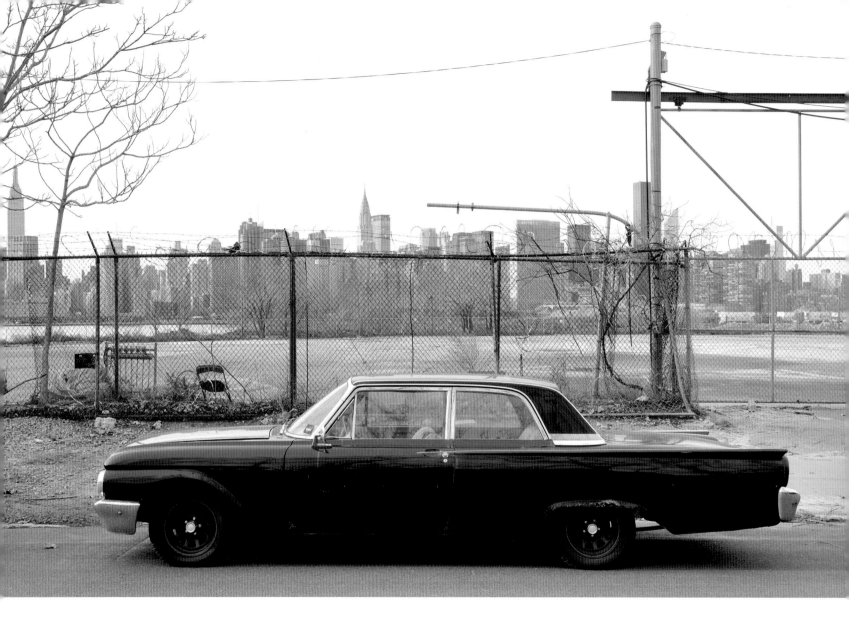

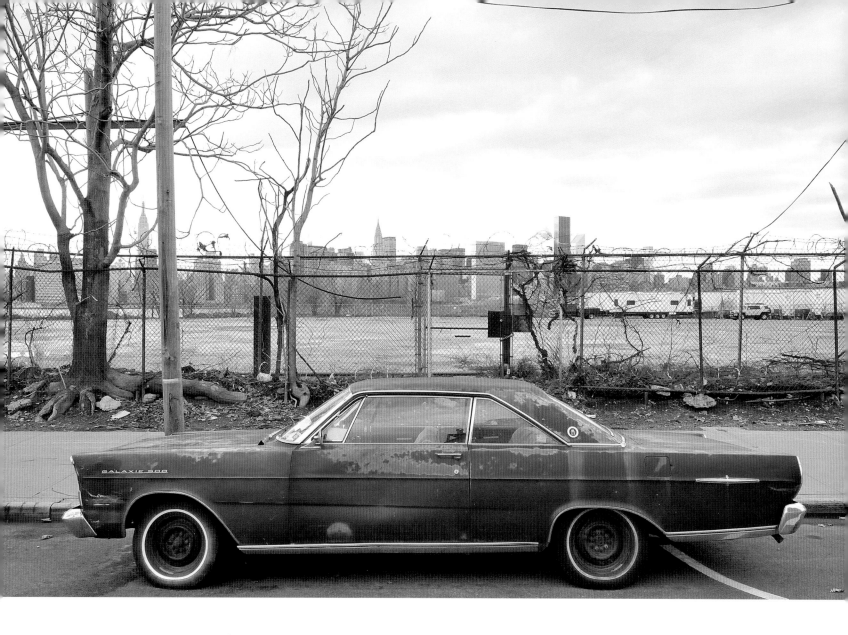

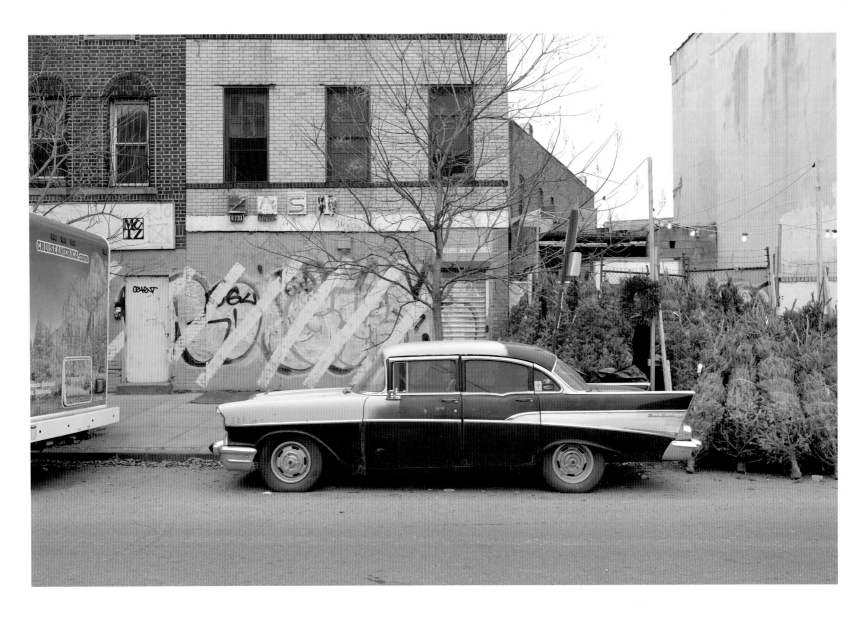

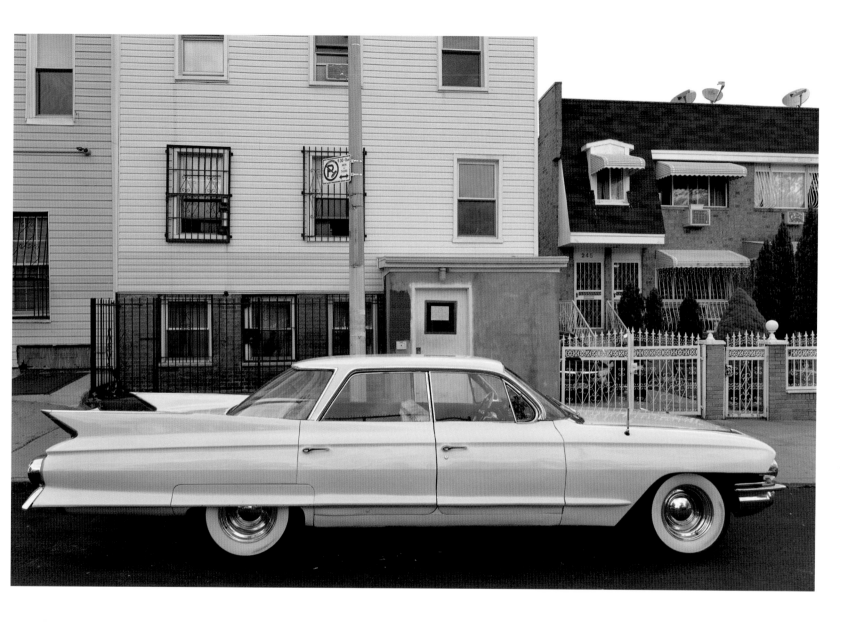

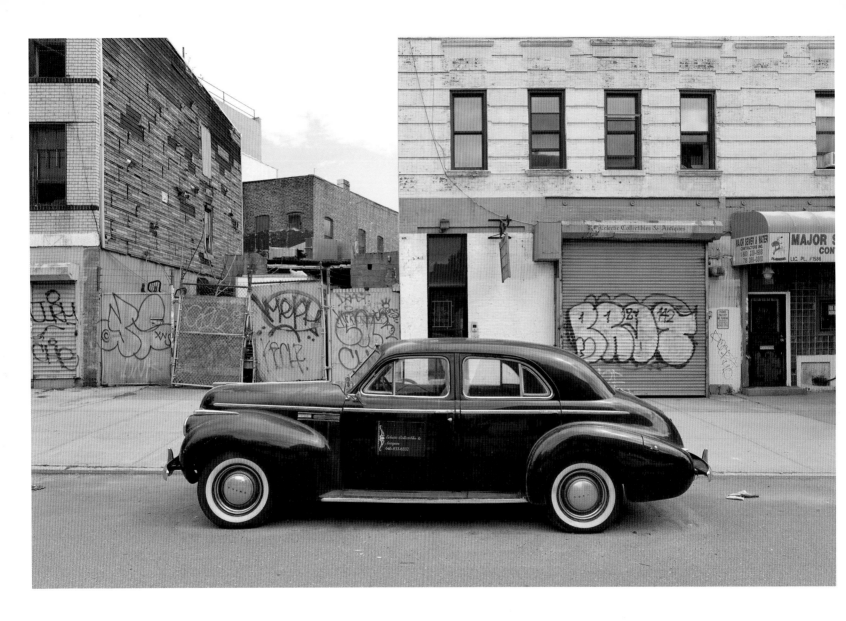

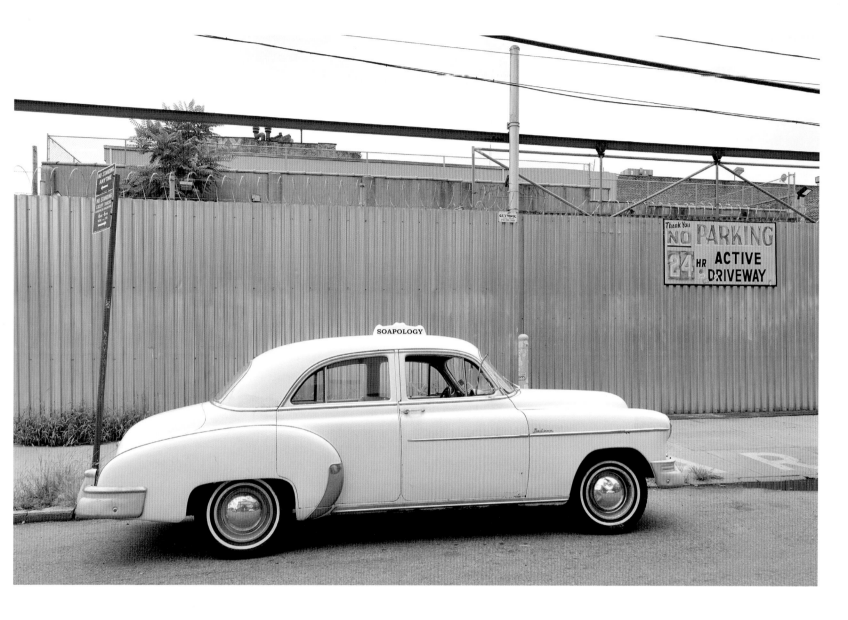

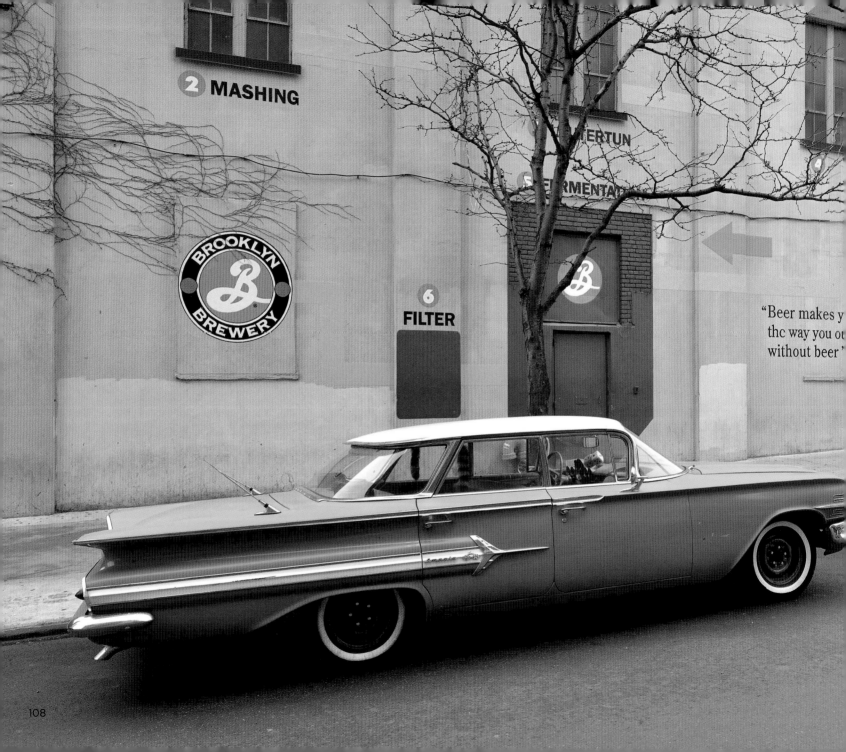

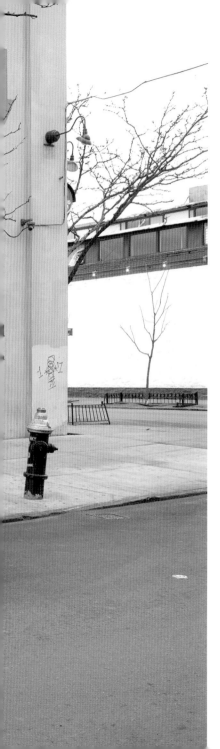

"BROOKLYN'S GOOD. BROOKLYN'S FUNKY. BROOKLYN'S HAPPENING."

WARIS DIRIE

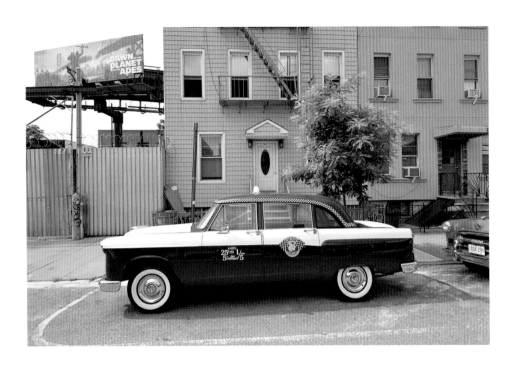

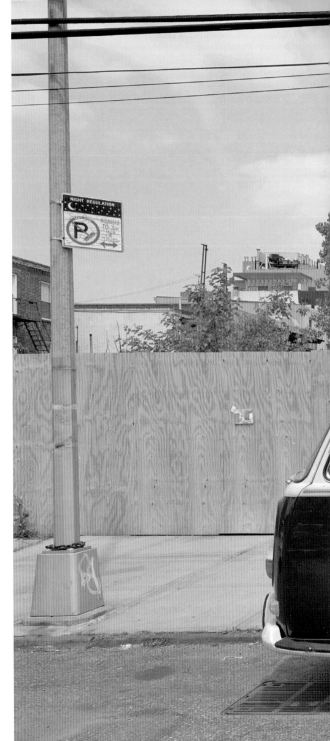

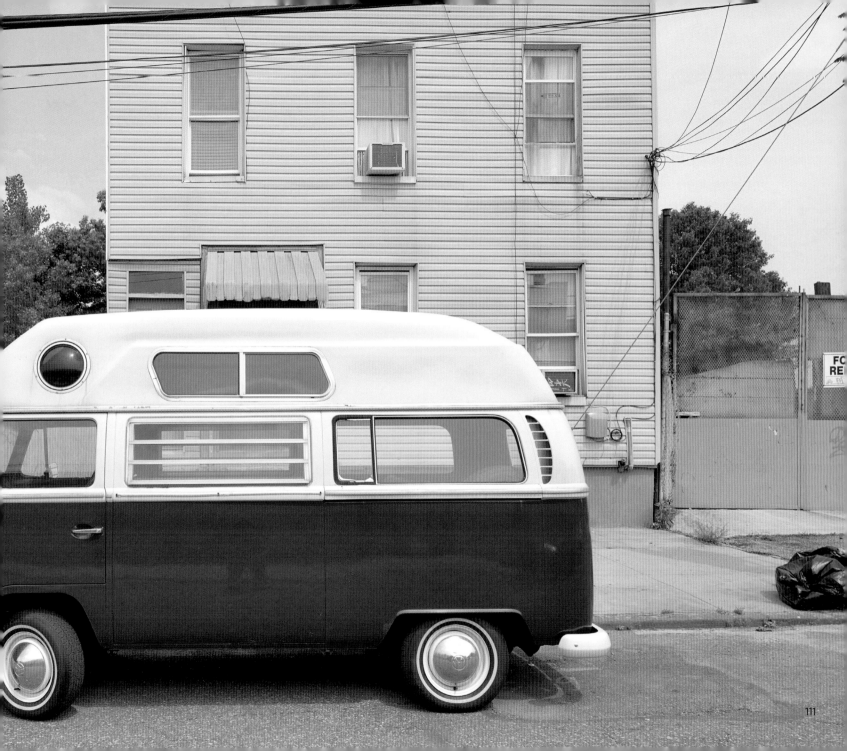

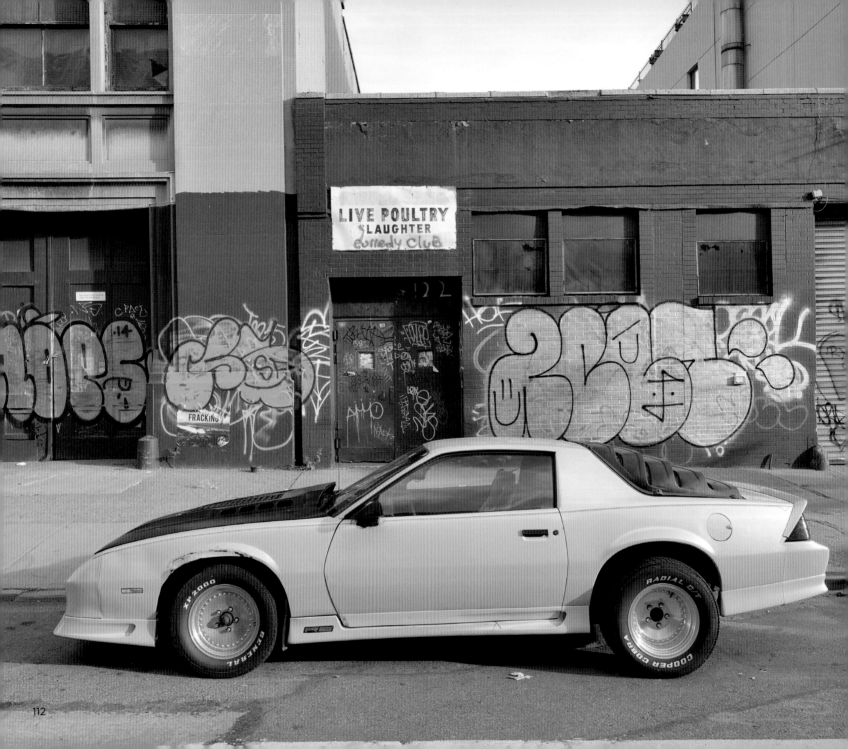

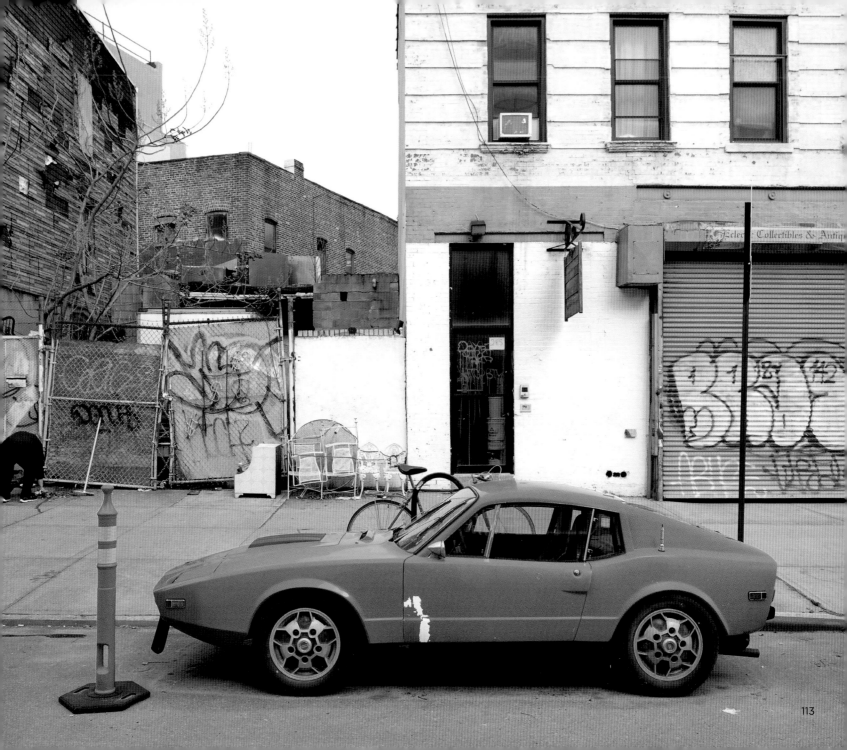

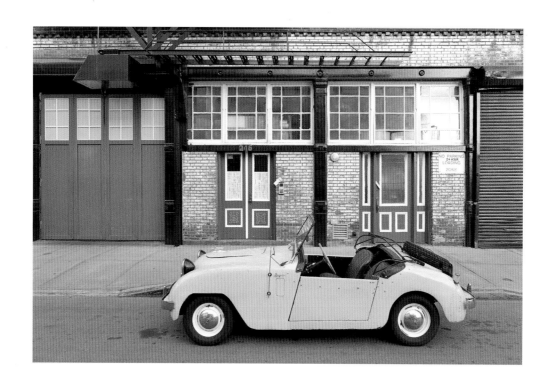

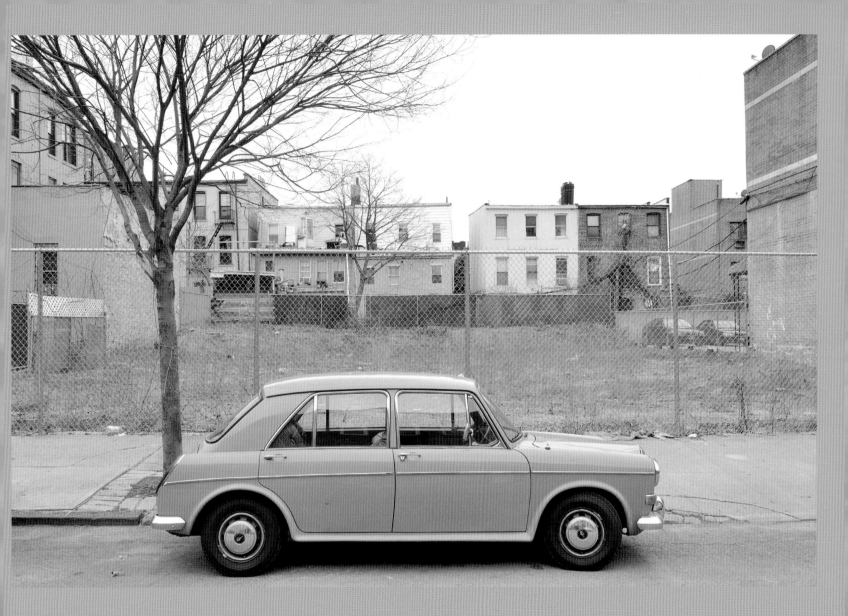

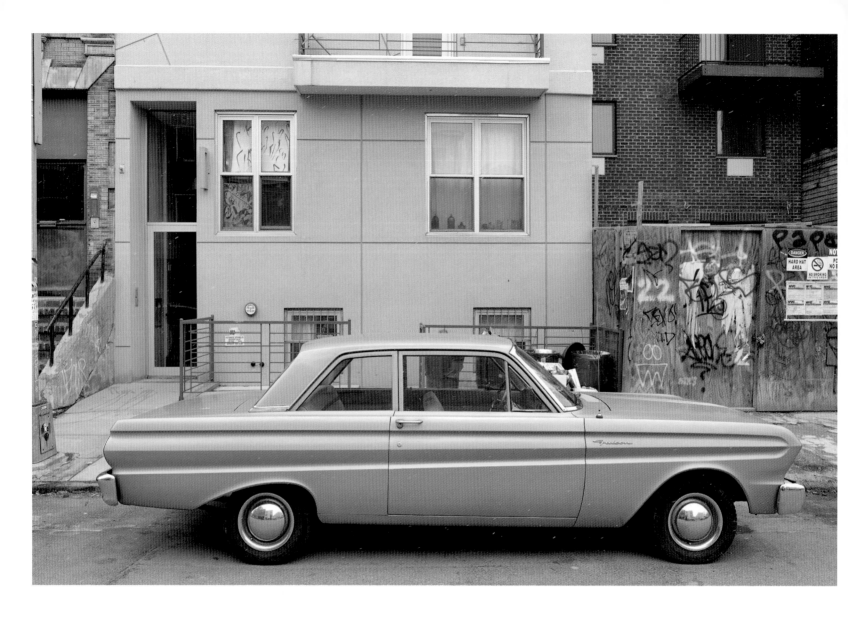

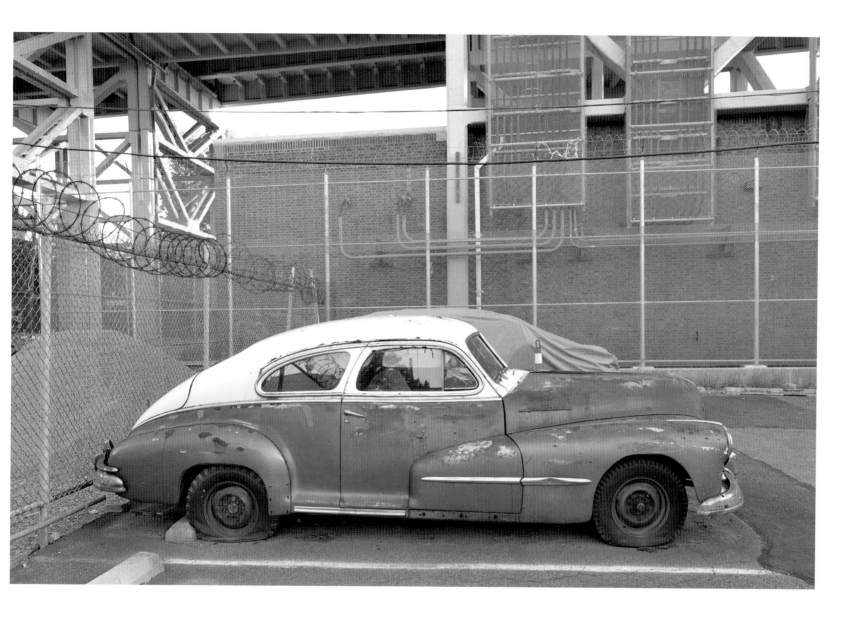

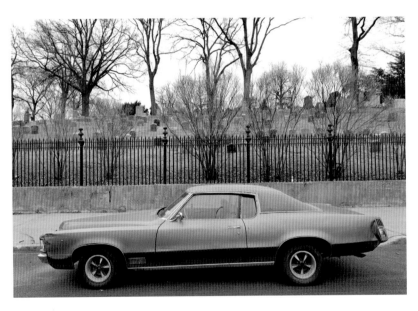
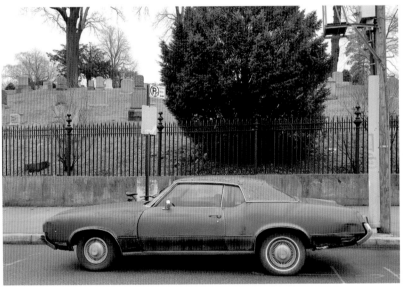

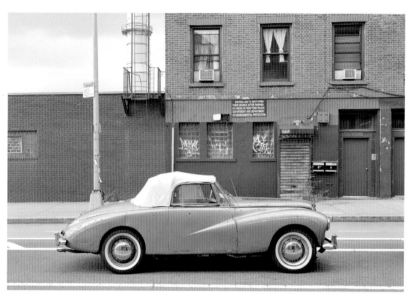
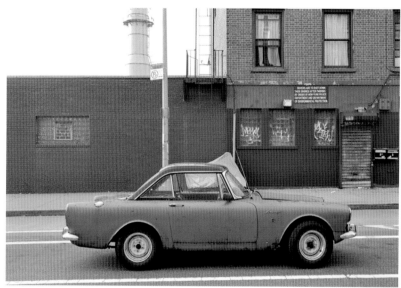

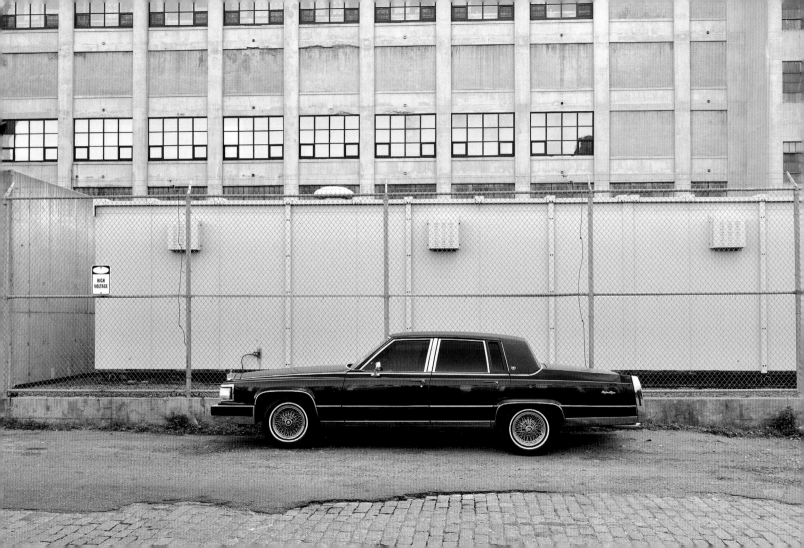

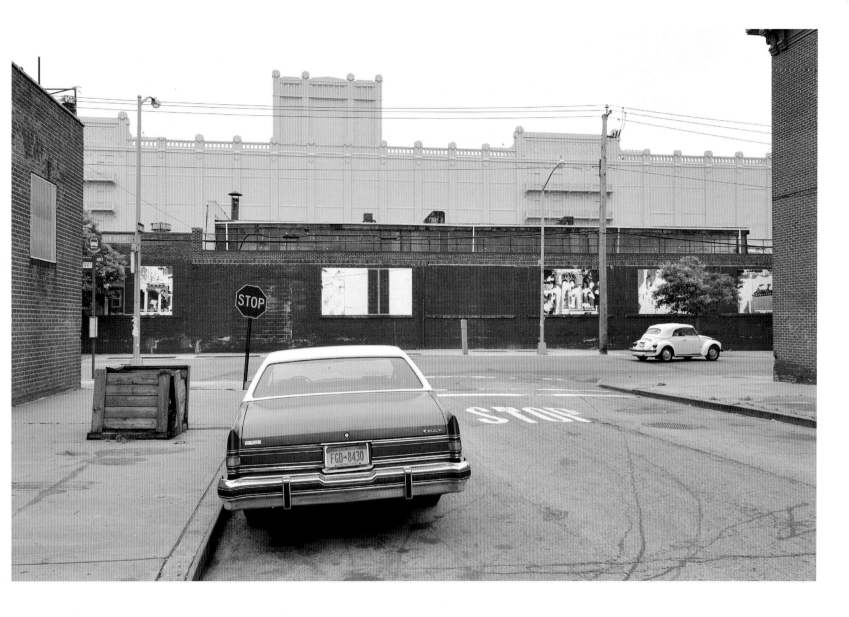

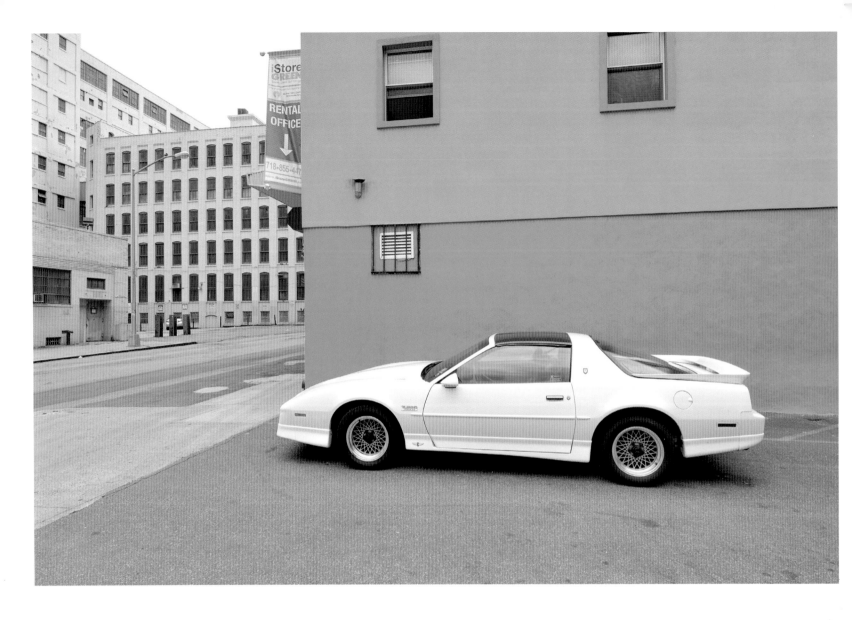

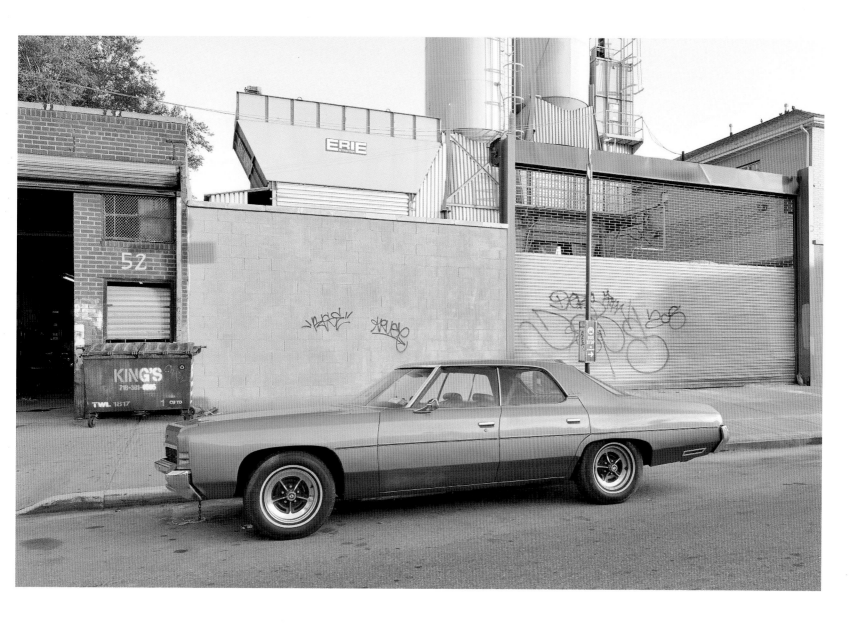

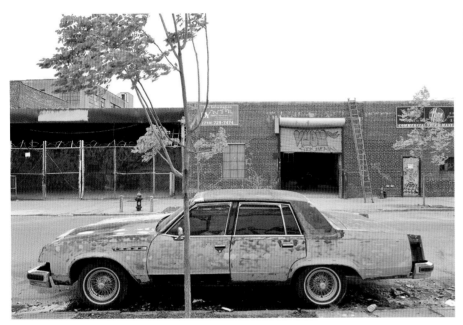

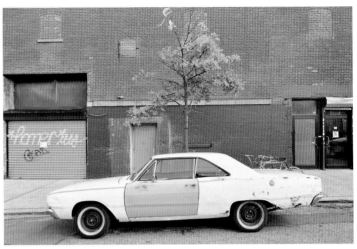

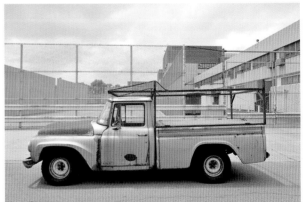

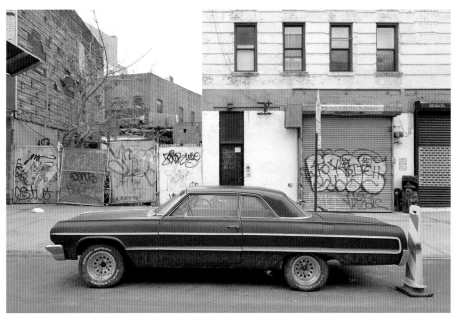

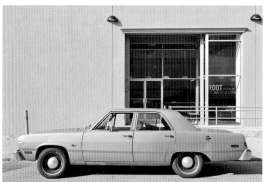

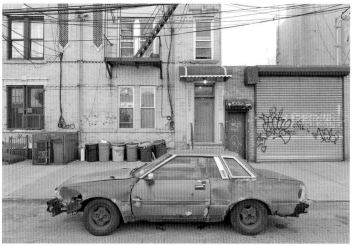

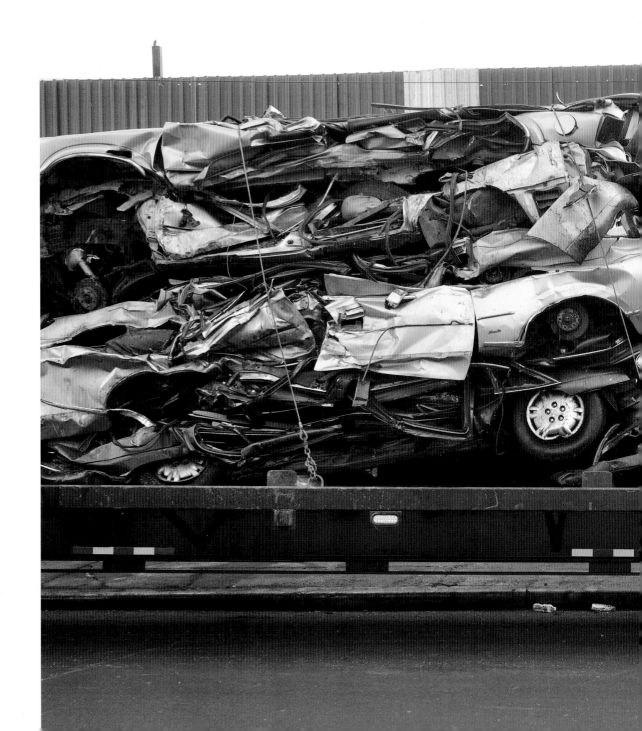

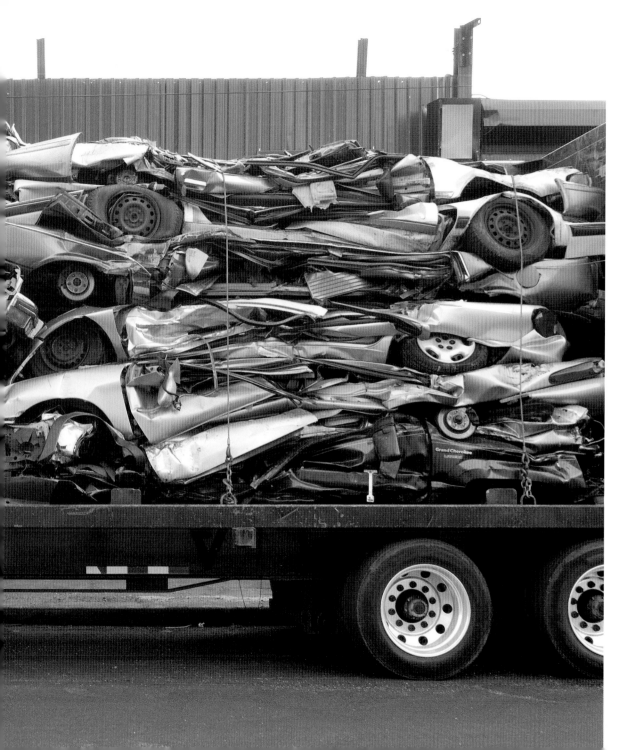

THE CARS

Published in 2018 by
Unicorn, an imprint of Unicorn
Publishing Group LLP
101 Wardour Street
London
W1F 0UG
www.unicornpublishing.org

Images © Douglas Ljungkvist
Introduction © Dean Johnson
Work © Unicorn Publishing Group

ISBN 978-1-911604-31-0

10 9 8 7 6 5 4 3 2 1

Designed by Matt Carr
Printed in India by Imprint Press